℗ pillsbury publications

Pillsbury's Bake Off Main Dish Cook Book

Shortcutted prize winning favorites...the best of all the Bake Offs

Dear Homemaker:

*It's no accident that the word "Casserole" comes
from "casa", meaning "home". Nothing says home
and home-cooking better than a savory casserole, with
its endless variety of flavor minglings and food
combinations. It is a category where the homemaker
can display great ingenuity and creativity.*

*In the last eighteen years of Bake Offs, many exciting
casserole ideas have been among the finalists and
winners. We have taken our favorites of these, and
brought the recipes up to date to meet the needs of
today's lady-in-the-kitchen. The original recipes have
been streamlined and short-cutted where possible.
In some instances, ingredients no longer available
have been substituted. But the good ideas are
here, and easier than ever to prepare. They run
the gamut from family fare to gourmet delights,
with a special section devoted to recipes
for larger groups.*

*There are one hundred and sixty-four recipes
in this book. We hope you will take
pleasure in preparing and enjoying them,
and perhaps include some of them
in your regular menu planning.*

Cordially yours,

Ann Pillsbury

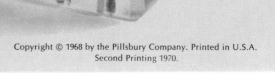

Contents

Pictured on Cover: Steak Bake Casserole, page 116

Basics

• A few "basics" for ready reference are essential when preparing main dishes. Here are the important "basics" for reference when preparing recipes in this book.

When a recipe calls for cooked chicken, you can use leftover chicken you may happen to have in the refrigerator, you can use canned chicken, or you can cook a fresh chicken . . . preferably a stewing chicken. Keep in mind that a 5-ounce can yields ⅔ cup cubed, cooked chicken; a 3 pound 4-ounce canned whole chicken yields about 2½ cups cubed chicken. A 5 pound stewing chicken yields 5 cups cubed or chopped cooked chicken, plus about 4 cups broth.

Stewed Chicken

4 to 5 pound cut up stewing chicken
4 cups water
1 onion, sliced
1 celery stalk, cut into pieces
2 or 3 peppercorns

Place all ingredients in large saucepan. Cover and simmer 2 to 3 hours until tender. Remove chicken, strain broth. When chicken is cool, remove skin and bones, cut into pieces. Cover and refrigerate. Use it within two days. If longer storage is desired, wrap it tightly in freezer foil and freeze.

Turkey may usually be substituted for chicken, if you have leftover turkey. Or you may find it convenient to cook a frozen boneless turkey roast for the recipe. A 3 pound roast yields about 5 cups chopped, cooked turkey.

The *ham* you use in the recipes in this book may be canned ham, fully cooked, ready-to-eat ham (which you may use without heating), or leftover baked ham.

Many grades of *ground meats* go under the banner of "ground beef." In your butcher's display, you may see plain ground beef, lean ground beef, ground chuck, ground round and ground sirloin. Any of these may be used in the recipes in this book that call for ground beef, but bear in mind that the more fat content in the ground beef, the more "pour-off" juice forms in cooking. This reduces the cooked quantity accordingly. Some recipes in this book specify lean ground beef. The excess fat is not drained in these recipes, so be sure to buy lean ground beef, ground chuck or ground round. Store ground beef lightly covered in the coldest part of your refrigerator, and use it within two days.

Flour keeps best in a covered canister. If you store it in the bag, keep it tightly closed. Pillsbury's Best All Purpose Flour has been used in developing the recipes in this book. To measure flour simply spoon lightly into your measuring cup and level it off with a knife.

When a Pillsbury flour sack is marked "Self-Rising", the leavening and salt are already in it. When you use this flour, you must omit baking powder and salt. Some recipes, however, need special adjustment.

Pastry

Single Crust	Double Crust
I cup Pillsbury's Best All Purpose Flour*	2 cups Pillsbury's Best All Purpose Flour*
½ teaspoon salt	I teaspoon salt
⅓ cup shortening	⅔ cup shortening
3 to 4 tablespoons cold water	5 to 7 tablespoons cold water

Combine flour and salt in mixing bowl. Cut in shortening using a pastry blender or knife until mixture is the size of small peas. Sprinkle water over mixture, a tablespoon at a time, while tossing and stirring lightly with fork.

Add water until dough is just moist enough to hold together. Form into a ball (2 balls for a double crust). Flatten each to ½-inch thickness on floured surface; smooth edges. Roll out to a circle I-inch larger than inverted 8 or 9-inch pie pan. Fold pastry in half, transfer to pie pan, unfold and fit loosely into pan, gently patting out any air pockets.

*For use with Pillsbury's Best Self-Rising Flour, omit salt.

<u>Unbaked Pastry Shell</u>: Prepare Single Crust as directed above. Fold edge to form a standing rim; flute. Pour in filling and bake as directed in recipe.

<u>Baked Pastry Shell</u>: Prepare as for Unbaked Pastry Shell. Prick bottom and sides generously with fork. Bake at 450° for 8 to I0 minutes until light golden brown.

<u>Double Crust Pastry</u>: Pour filling into bottom crust. Roll out top crust; cut slits for escape of steam. Place top crust over filling. Fold top crust under bottom crust. Seal; flute edge.

<u>Tip:</u> Or, use Pillsbury Butterflake Recipe Pie Crust Mix or Pillsbury Flaky Pie Crust Sticks. Prepare as directed on package for single or double crust pie.

Main-dish Dishes

● A true casserole-enthusiast picks her dish with as much care as she chooses her recipe. Below are some representative type dishes for which the recipes in this book are designed.

Did you know that you can often BROWN YOUR MEAT in the same casserole dish in which you bake it and bring it to the table?

Shallow Casseroles. *Faster-cooking, because they are only 1½-inches deep, these pans (sometimes used for baking) come in a variety of sizes of squares and rectangles.*

Deep Casseroles. *These deep, roomy one to three-quart casseroles take a little longer than shallow pans to heat through the center and cook the topping.*

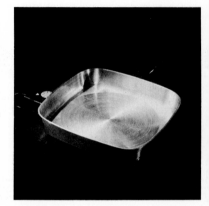

Electric Skillet. *With this, you can brown and simmer without constant watching. Just set the dial to the right temperature. (Mixtures boil at 212°F.) Good for deep-fat frying small amounts, too.*

Earthenware Casseroles. *Their peasant charm enhances many a main dish, in either deep or shallow versions. Be careful about sudden changes from cold to hot.*

Ceramic Casseroles. *Deep or shallow, ceramic is ideal for do-aheads and freezing. They go from refrigerator or freezer directly to your oven without breaking.*

Deep-Fat Fryer. *Ideal for deep-fat frying, and can also be used for soups and stews on lower temperature. A heavy saucepan on a controlled heat burner also makes a good deep-fat fryer.*

It's the new oven method of browning and cooking, which makes it no longer necessary to use the skillet first. Many of the recipes in this book call for it.

When you don't know the YIELD of a casserole dish, simply measure it with cups of water — four cups to a quart, of course.

A word about TEFLON pans. Remember that they do not require greasing unless the mixture is high in sugar . . . a cake, for instance. Also, remember that mixtures baked directly on teflon brown slightly faster, so keep an eye on the clock.

Dutch Oven. *A deep, heavy saucepan, ideal for browning meats and then simmering. They are very heavy and hold the heat well without scorching.*

Chafing Dish. *These come to the table and keep foods hot in style, without sticking. The secret is an underpan of hot water, directly over a burner.*

Fondue Pot. *For Cheese Fondue choose an earthenware pot; for Beef Fondue, a metal pot is best for keeping the oil at a high temperature. The burner keeps the food hot at the table.*

Cookie Sheets. *Usually sideless, because they are for foods that hold their shape. A 15x10-inch roll pan is similar but has 1-inch sides.*

Soufflé Dishes. *These deep, straight-sided dishes allow your soufflé mixture to rise to crowning heights, more than an ordinary deep casserole would.*

Pizza Pan. *Round with a slight rim. Without this, you can make round pizza on a cookie sheet. Just form a standing rim along the edge of the dough, to hold the filling.*

Tips

Cook's Choice The real success of any meal happens before you pull out a pan or measure a single ingredient. It's in the planning. Mix and vary the colors, shapes, flavors, textures and temperatures of the foods in your meal, and you'll create excitement, eye appeal and appetite. Let COLORS accent each other: a colorful vegetable salad with a plain-jane main dish; a muted casserole with cheerful little garnishes. Take SHAPE into consideration and strive for variety on the plate. Avoid repetition such as meat-balls, Brussels-sprouts and tiny new potatoes together. Meat balls would be better, shape-wise, with mashed potatoes and string beans. Let FLAVORS compliment each other. Combine tart, sweet and spicy foods with bland ones for balance. Once a flavor is featured in a meal (tomato juice, for instance), don't bring it back for a re-run in the salad or the aspic. Play TEXTURES against each other with crisp salads accompanying cushiony casseroles, crunchy toppings on soft mixtures. Let your combinations include creamed foods, buttered and raw. TEMPERATURE, too, is part of the picture. Cold and hot foods make great plate-mates, and you may want to use a cool refreshing dessert after a heavy, hot meal.

Keeping Casseroles Many casserole dishes can be prepared (or partly prepared) early in the day or even the night before. They are then REFRIGERATED and ready to pop into the oven. Do-ahead dishes are noted in the recipes in this book.

Freezing casserole dishes is not always time-saving. Some foods take less time to prepare fresh than frozen. However, a freezer stocked with two or three ready-prepared casseroles can be a boon for unexpected guests or quick, busy-day meals. Casserole dishes and stews FREEZE BEST if they are made with enough sauce so that the solid pieces are completely covered during freezing. Take care not to over-cook them. Cool thoroughly, cover and seal with foil before freezing. THAW AND HEAT frozen casseroles in a hot, 400° to 450° oven. When casseroles call for a biscuit or other leavened topping, it's a good idea to prepare and freeze only the bottom portion, heat it thoroughly and prepare and add the topping just before serving. Be sure the casserole is thoroughly thawed and heated through before you add the topping.

Terms

Directions:

Baste . . . During cooking, to spoon liquid or fat over it.

Blend . . . Combine two or more ingredients thoroughly.

Boil . . . To heat until bubbles constantly break the surface.

Bone . . . To remove the bone from meat, fish or poultry.

Broil . . . To cook under direct heat.

Brown . . . To make food brown either in a small amount of hot fat on top of the range, or by exposing it to dry heat in the oven.

Chop . . . To cut into small pieces with a knife or other cutting device.

Coat . . . To cover entire surface with a mixture such as seasoned flour, fine crumbs, batter, etc.

Cube . . . To cut into small cubes of a regular size. (See dice)

Cut in . . . To use two knives, pastry blender or fork to distribute shortening through dry ingredients, leaving it in small particles.

Deep-fat Fry . . . To cook in deep fat which completely covers the food being prepared.

Dice . . . To cut into very small cubes.

Flake . . . To break into small pieces, usually with a fork.

Fold . . . To combine a solid ingredient with a delicate substance (egg white or whipped cream) without air loss. Insert spoon or spatula down through the middle of mixture, across bottom, bring it up and "fold" over on top. Continue until all is evenly mixed.

Grate . . . To rub a food against a grater to form small particles.

Knead . . . To work dough by repeatedly stretching it with the hands, folding it over and pressing it with the knuckles or "heel" of the hand.

Mince . . . To chop very fine.

Pan-broil . . . To cook meat uncovered in a skillet, turning frequently, and pouring off excess fat.

Pare . . . To remove peeling with a knife.

Saute . . . To cook in a skillet in a small amount of fat.

Scald . . . To heat just below the boiling point. Also to pour boiling water over food or to dip food briefly into boiling water.

Shred . . . To tear or cut into thin pieces.

Simmer . . . To cook just below the boiling point so that tiny bubbles form on the bottom or sides of pan.

Ingredients:

Eggs, slightly beaten . . . Beaten just enough to mix both yolk and white.

Eggs, well beaten . . . Beaten with rotary beater until light and foamy.

Broth . . . The water in which meat or vegetables have been cooked, now containing juices and fats.

Clove of garlic . . . One section of the garlic bulb.

Bread cubes, soft . . . Cubes made from fresh or day-old bread.

Bread cubes, dry . . . Cubes made from air-dried or toasted bread. May be dried or toasted after cutting into cubes.

Bread crumbs, dry . . . Crumbs made from air-dried or toasted bread.

Yeast, active dry . . . Granulated, and stays fresh on the cupboard shelf.

Yeast, compressed . . . In cake form, and will keep for several weeks in refrigerator.

Measures

Food	Quantity	Yields
Almonds	4 oz.	I cup diced roasted or I cup slivered
Apples	I medium	I cup chopped
Bread	3 to 4 slices	I cup dry bread crumbs
	I slice	¾ cup soft bread cubes or ¾ cup dry bread cubes
Cabbage	I pound	4 cups shredded cabbage
Celery	2 medium stalks	I cup sliced celery or I cup chopped celery
Cheese	4 oz. (¼ pound)	I cup shredded cheese
Cheese, cream	3 oz.	6 tablespoons
Cracker crumbs, soda	20 crackers	I cup soda cracker crumbs
Green pepper	I medium	I cup chopped green pepper
Mushrooms	½ pound fresh or I pint fresh	3 (4-oz.) cans stems and pieces
Onion	I medium	I cup chopped
Potatoes	I small	I cup cubed potato

SUBSTITUTIONS

Chives . . . I tablespoon freeze-dried or frozen = I tablespoon chopped fresh

Garlic . . . ⅛ teaspoon garlic powder or ½ teaspoon garlic salt = I medium clove garlic

Onion . . . I tablespoon instant minced = ⅓ cup chopped fresh

I tablespoon dried onion flakes = ¼ cup chopped fresh

I tablespoon onion salt = ¼ cup chopped fresh

Parsley . . . I tablespoon dried parsley flakes = 3 tablespoons chopped fresh parsley

Sweet pepper . . . I tablespoon sweet pepper flakes = 2 tablespoons chopped fresh green and red peppers

Buttermilk . . . I tablespoon vinegar plus milk to make I cup = I cup buttermilk or sour milk

CAN SIZES

Size	Weight	Approximate Cups
4 oz.	4 oz.	½ cup
8 oz.	8 oz.	I cup
picnic	10½-12 oz.	1¼ cups
12 oz. (vacuum)	12 oz.	1½ cups
#300	14-16 oz.	1¾ cups
#303	16-17 oz.	2 cups
#2	I lb. 4 oz. or I pt. 2 fl. oz.	2½ cups
#2½	I lb. 13 oz.	3½ cups
#3	3 lb. 3 oz. or I qt. 14 fl. oz.	5¾ cups
#10	6½-7 lb. 5 oz.	12-13 cups

Great Ground Beef Recipes

• Be it ever so humble, ground beef is a favorite of young and old alike. Not the least of its talents is its versatility. It can be coupled with vegetables or quick-breads (or both), enhanced with common or exotic flavorings; it can be shaped or crumbled, baked or fried, served plain or fancy, and it's always different. If you think you've done everything possible with ground beef, look over the recipes on the following pages. You're sure to find a new idea.

Hungry Boys' Casserole

Biscuits cut with doughnut cutter and filled with bean-meat filling mixture. Complete in an hour and a quarter.

Hungry Boys' Casserole

½ cup chopped celery
¼ cup chopped onion
¼ cup chopped green pepper
 I pound lean ground beef
 I-pound can pork and beans
¼ cup catsup
¼ cup water
½ teaspoon salt
½ teaspoon garlic salt

Biscuits

 I cup Pillsbury's Best All Purpose Flour*
I½ teaspoons baking powder
½ teaspoon salt
⅓ cup.milk
 3 tablespoons oil
 4 drops yellow food coloring

OVEN 425°   4 TO 5 SERVINGS

Sprinkle celery, onion and green pepper in bottom of 8-inch baking dish. Crumble ground beef on top. Bake uncovered at 425° for 20 minutes. Remove from oven. Stir in pork and beans, catsup, water, salt and garlic salt until well blended. Reserve ½ cup of bean-meat mixture. Return casserole to oven for 10 minutes while preparing Biscuits. Arrange Biscuits without centers on casserole. Spoon reserved bean-meat filling in hole of each Biscuit. Top with the biscuit holes. Bake at 425° for 15 to 20 minutes until golden brown.

Biscuits: Combine flour, baking powder and salt in mixing bowl. Combine milk, oil and food coloring. Add to dry ingredients all at once stirring until dough clings together. Knead on floured surface 8 times. Roll out to ¼-inch thickness. Cut with doughnut cutter saving holes.

*For use with Pillsbury's Best Self-Rising Flour, omit baking powder and salt.

Hearty main dish, with meat, vegetables and distinctive topping. Start this an hour before serving time.

Easy Stroganoff Casserole

 I pound lean ground beef
⅓ cup chopped onion
 2 tablespoons flour
10¾-ounce can condensed vegetable soup
 4-ounce can mushroom stems and pieces, drained
¾ cup dairy sour cream
 2 tablespoons dried parsley flakes
 I teaspoon Worcestershire sauce
½ teaspoon garlic salt
½ teaspoon salt
⅛ teaspoon pepper
 Poppy seed

Drop Biscuits

 I cup Pillsbury's Best All Purpose Flour*
I½ teaspoons baking powder
½ teaspoon salt
½ teaspoon paprika
¼ teaspoon celery seed
½ cup milk
 3 tablespoons cooking oil

OVEN 425°   6 TO 8 SERVINGS

Combine ground beef and onion in 2-quart casserole. Bake uncovered at 425° for 20 minutes. Remove from oven; drain. Stir in flour. Blend in remaining ingredients except poppy seed. Drop Biscuits by tablespoonfuls onto meat mixture. Sprinkle with poppy seed. Bake at 425° for 30 to 35 minutes.

Drop Biscuits: Combine flour, baking powder, salt, paprika and celery seed. Combine milk and oil. Add to dry ingredients all at once. Stir only until moistened.

*For use with Pillsbury's Best Self-Rising Flour, omit baking powder and salt.

A hot dish for a cold night, and the pinwheel biscuits make it fancy. Ready for the table in about an hour and a quarter.

Savory Meatball Casserole

    1 pound lean ground beef
    ¼ pound pork sausage
    ½ cup dry bread crumbs or soda cracker
        crumbs
    1 tablespoon instant minced onion
    1 teaspoon chili powder
    ⅛ teaspoon pepper
    1 egg
    10½-ounce can condensed cream of
        mushroom soup
    10½-ounce can condensed cream of celery
        soup

Biscuits

    1½ cups Pillsbury's Best All Purpose Flour*
    1 tablespoon baking powder
    ½ teaspoon chili powder
    ¼ teaspoon salt
    ⅓ cup milk
    ⅓ cup cooking oil
    1 egg
    1 cup shredded American cheese
    1 tablespoon dried parsley flakes or
        3 tablespoons chopped fresh parsley

OVEN 425°   6 SERVINGS

Combine ground beef, pork sausage, bread crumbs, onion, chili powder, pepper and egg. Shape by tablespoonfuls into meatballs. Place in greased 2-quart casserole. Bake uncovered at 425° for 20 minutes. Remove from oven. Drain off excess fat. Add mushroom and celery soups; stir just to blend. Place Biscuits cut-side up on top of meat mixture. Bake at 425° for 30 to 35 minutes.

Biscuits: Combine dry ingredients. Blend milk, oil and egg together. Add to dry ingredients. Stir just until moistened. Knead lightly on floured surface 8 times. Roll out to a 12-inch square. Sprinkle with cheese and parsley. Roll up; seal edges by pinching together. Cut into 12 slices.

Tips: For a quick and easy topping, use 1 can Pillsbury Refrigerated Quick Crescent Dinner Rolls. Open can; unroll dough to form 4 rectangles. Mix together the cheese and parsley and ½ teaspoon chili powder. Sprinkle over dough. Roll up each of the 4 rectangles. Pinch
to seal edges. Cut each into 4 slices. Place on top of hot meatball mixture. Bake at 400° for 30 to 35 minutes.

For ease in cutting cheese roll, use a piece of heavy thread. Place thread around roll; cross ends over top; pull.

*For use with Pillsbury's Best Self-Rising Flour, omit baking powder and salt.

Barbecued beef balls with drop biscuits in between. Ready for ranchhands in an hour.

Rancho Beef Bake

    1-pound can beans in barbecue sauce
    1-pound can tomatoes
    1 pound lean ground beef
    ½ cup Pillsbury Hungry Jack Mashed
        Potato Flakes or soda cracker crumbs
    1 packet onion soup mix
    1 egg
    ¼ cup catsup
    ¼ teaspoon pepper

Drop Biscuits

    1 cup Pillsbury's Best All Purpose Flour*
    1½ teaspoons baking powder
    ¼ teaspoon salt
    ½ cup milk
    3 tablespoons cooking oil

OVEN 400°   6 SERVINGS

Combine beans and tomatoes in 9-inch square baking dish; spread evenly. Combine ground beef, potato flakes, ¼ cup onion soup mix, egg, catsup and pepper in mixing bowl. Shape into twenty-one 1½-inch meatballs. Arrange in three rows lengthwise on top of beans. Bake uncovered at 400° for 20 minutes. Remove from oven. Drop Biscuits by tablespoonfuls into 2 rows between meatballs. Bake at 400° for 20 to 25 minutes longer.

Drop Biscuits: Combine dry ingredients with remainder of onion soup mix in mixing bowl. Combine milk and oil; add all at once stirring only until moistened.

*For use with Pillsbury's Best Self-Rising Flour, omit baking powder and salt.

A simple stroganoff with potato-drop biscuit topping. Dinner can be ready in an hour.

Potato Pan Burger

    I pound lean ground beef
    I package Pillsbury Brown Gravy mix
10½-ounce can condensed cream of
      mushroom soup
    ¾ cup dairy sour cream
    ¼ cup water
    I tablespoon catsup

Topping
    I cup Pillsbury Hungry Jack Mashed
     Potato Flakes
    I cup Pillsbury's Best All Purpose Flour*
    2 teaspoons baking powder
    ½ teaspoon salt
    ¾ cup milk
    2 tablespoons cooking oil
    I egg

OVEN 450°   5 TO 6 SERVINGS

Place ground beef in 2-quart casserole. Break into small pieces. Bake at 450° for 20 minutes. Drain. Add gravy mix, mushroom soup, sour cream, water and catsup. Mix well. Drop Topping by tablespoonfuls around edge of casserole. Sprinkle with additional potato flakes. Bake at 450° for 25 to 30 minutes.

Topping: Combine potato flakes, flour, baking powder and salt in mixing bowl. Combine milk, oil and egg; add to dry ingredients all at once, stirring until all ingredients are moistened.

Tip: Prepare meat mixture ahead. Cover and refrigerate. Prepare Topping just before baking and bake at 425° for 35 to 40 minutes.

*For use with Pillsbury's Best Self-Rising Flour, decrease salt to ¼ teaspoon and omit baking powder.

The biscuits on this appetizing casserole each contain a cheese surprise. You can have this ready to serve in an hour.

Cheeseburger Casserole

    I pound lean ground beef
    ⅓ cup chopped onion
10¾-ounce can condensed tomato soup
    8-ounce can peas, drained
    I teaspoon Worcestershire sauce
    ½ teaspoon salt
    ⅛ teaspoon pepper

Biscuits
    I cup Pillsbury's Best All Purpose Flour*
    1½ teaspoons baking powder
    ¼ teaspoon salt
    ¼ cup plus 2 tablespoons milk
    2 tablespoons cooking oil
    8 (½-inch) cubes American or Cheddar
     cheese

OVEN 425°   5 TO 6 SERVINGS

Combine ground beef and onion in 1½-quart casserole. Bake at 425° for 20 minutes. Drain. Add tomato soup, peas, Worcestershire sauce, salt and pepper. Place Biscuits seam-side down on casserole. Bake at 425° for 25 to 30 minutes.

Biscuits: Combine dry ingredients in mixing bowl. Combine milk and cooking oil. Add to dry ingredients all at once, stirring until dough clings together. Knead lightly on floured surface 8 times. Divide into 8 equal portions. Mold each portion around a cheese cube, pinching to seal edges.

Tips: Instead of making Biscuits, use I can Pillsbury Refrigerated Country Style or Buttermilk Biscuits molding each biscuit around a cheese cube. Place on hot casserole. Bake at 400° for 25 to 30 minutes.

Savory beef and frankfurters are crowned with flavorful yeast rolls. Allow up to one and a half hours for total preparation.

Beef Burger Bar-B-Que

    I package active dry yeast
    ¼ cup warm water
10½-ounce can condensed onion soup
    I tablespoon sugar
    2 tablespoons cooking oil
    ½ teaspoon salt
    I egg
1½ to 1¾ cups Pillsbury's Best All
      Purpose Flour*
      Celery seed

Filling

    I pound lean ground beef
    ½ pound frankfurters, cut into ¼-inch
      diagonal slices
    ¼ cup barbecue sauce
    ¼ cup water
    I tablespoon sugar

OVEN 375°   6 SERVINGS

Add yeast to warm water in small mixer bowl. Measure ¼ cup liquid from can of onion soup. Blend into yeast along with sugar, cooking oil, salt and egg. Add I cup flour; beat at medium speed one minute. Gradually stir in remaining flour to form a soft dough. Cover; let rise in warm place 45 minutes.

While dough is rising, prepare Filling by breaking ground beef into small pieces in 9-inch square pan. Bake at 375° for 30 minutes. Remove from oven. Drain off excess fat. Add frankfurters, barbecue sauce, water, sugar and remainder of onion soup. Mix well. Return to oven until yeast dough is ready.

After yeast dough has risen, beat down. Drop tablespoonfuls on top of hot meat mixture. Sprinkle with celery seed. Let rise for I5 minutes. Bake at 375° for I5 to 20 minutes or until golden brown.

*For use with Pillsbury's Best Self-Rising Flour, omit salt.

*HIGH ALTITUDE ADJUSTMENT — 5,200 FEET.
During first rising time, decrease rising time from 45 minutes to 30 minutes.*

The unusual touch of nutmeg and cinnamon make this meat pie distinctive. Ready in an hour and a quarter.

Heirloom Meat Pie

I recipe Double-Crust Pastry, see page 5

    I egg
    I pound lean ground beef
 ⅓ cup soda cracker crumbs
 ¼ cup milk
 ¼ cup tomato paste
  2 tablespoons instant minced onion
  I tablespoon sweet pepper flakes
I½ teaspoons salt
 ¼ teaspoon cinnamon
 ¼ teaspoon nutmeg

Vegetable Sauce

I0½-ounce can condensed cream of
    celery soup
  8-ounce can mixed vegetables, drained
 ½ cup milk
 ½ teaspoon dry mustard

OVEN 425°   5 TO 6 SERVINGS

Combine egg, ground beef, cracker crumbs, milk, tomato paste, onion, pepper flakes, salt, cinnamon and nutmeg. Turn into 9-inch pastry-lined pie pan. Roll out top crust; cut slits to let steam escape. Place over Filling; seal and flute. Bake at 425° for 30 to 35 minutes. Serve hot with Vegetable Sauce.

Vegetable Sauce: Blend soup, mixed vegetables, milk and dry mustard in saucepan. Heat thoroughly. If a thinner sauce is desired, add more milk.

Tips: If desired, use single crust and top with ½ cup crushed cereal combined with 2 tablespoons melted butter.

Under the attractive pastry-ring topping are hearty meatballs studded with cheese cubes. Takes about two hours.

Barbecue Meatball Pie

I recipe Double-Crust Pastry, see page 5

    I egg
    I pound lean ground beef
 I½ teaspoons salt
 ⅛ teaspoon pepper
 ¼ cup quick-cooking rolled oats
  I cup (¼-inch cubes) American cheese
  4 drops liquid smoke, if desired

Tomato Sauce

  8-ounce can stewed tomatoes
  7-ounce can whole kernel corn with sweet
    peppers, drained
  2 tablespoons flour
  I teaspoon instant minced onion
  2 tablespoons barbecue sauce

OVEN 425°   5 TO 6 SERVINGS

Combine egg, ground beef, salt, pepper, oats, cheese and liquid smoke. Form into 18 small meatballs. Place in 9-inch pastry-lined pie pan. Top with Tomato Sauce. Roll out remaining pastry. Cut into 3-inch rings. Place around edge of pie. Bake at 425° for 10 minutes, then at 375° for 35 to 45 minutes until crust is golden brown. Let stand 5 to 10 minutes before serving.

Tomato Sauce: Combine tomatoes, corn, flour, onion and barbecue sauce; mix well.

Tip: If a smoky flavor is desired in the pastry, add 4 drops liquid smoke to water in preparation.

Experiment with herbs and spices, seasoning salts, horseradish and mustard when you are putting together ingredients.

Swedish Meatball Dinner

I medium onion, sliced
½ pound lean ground beef
I egg
¼ cup dry bread crumbs or soda cracker
    crumbs
2 tablespoons milk
½ teaspoon salt
¼ teaspoon basil
    Dash of pepper
10¾-ounce can condensed tomato soup
    I-pound can mixed vegetables, undrained
    I teaspoon Worchestershire sauce

<u>Crust</u>
¾ cup Pillsbury's Best All Purpose Flour*
I tablespoon grated Parmesan cheese
½ teaspoon dried parsley flakes
¼ teaspoon salt
⅛ teaspoon dill seed
¼ cup shortening
2 to 3 tablespoons milk

OVEN 425°   4 TO 5 SERVINGS

Arrange onion slices on bottom of 8-inch square baking dish. Combine ground beef, egg, bread crumbs, milk, salt, basil and pepper. Shape into I-inch meatballs. Place on top of onion slices. Bake at 425° for 20 minutes. Remove from oven. Add tomato soup, mixed vegetables and Worcestershire sauce. Stir just to blend. Arrange Crust on meat mixture. Sprinkle with additional Parmesan cheese. Bake at 425° for 30 to 35 minutes.

Crust: Combine flour, Parmesan cheese, parsley, salt and dill seed in mixing bowl. Cut in shortening until particles are the size of small peas. Add milk and stir until dough clings together. Roll out on floured surface to 8-inch square. Cut into 2-inch squares or triangles if desired.

Tips: Substitute other vegetables for mixed vegetables using I cup vegetables and ⅔ cup liquid or water.

To make ahead, prepare meat mixture. Cover and store in refrigerator. Prepare Crust. Cut into squares or triangles and wrap in plastic wrap and refrigerate. Just before baking arrange Crust on meat mixture. Bake at 425° for 35 to 40 minutes.

*For use with Pillsbury's Best Self-Rising Flour, omit salt.

Flavorful pastry squares cover saucy meatballs and vegetables. Make it, bake it in an hour and a quarter.

An easy work of art, with fresh-sliced tomatoes and cheese wedges topping it all. About an hour to make and bake.

Tomato Cheeseburger Pie

8 or 9-inch Unbaked Pastry Shell, see page 5
I egg
I pound lean ground beef
I cup shredded Cheddar cheese
½ cup soda cracker crumbs
¼ cup barbecue sauce
I teaspoon instant minced onion
I teaspoon salt
⅛ teaspoon pepper
6 slices fresh tomato or 3 well-drained
    canned tomatoes, cut into halves
6 wedge-shaped slices Cheddar or
    American cheese

OVEN 425°   6 SERVINGS

Combine egg, ground beef, shredded cheese, cracker crumbs, barbecue sauce, onion, salt and pepper in mixing bowl. Press firmly into Unbaked Pastry Shell. Place tomatoes on top. Bake at 425° for 25 to 30 minutes. Remove from oven. Place cheese wedges over tomato slices and return to oven to melt cheese, about I minute.

Mexicali Meat Pie

8 or 9-inch Unbaked Pastry Shell, see page 5

Filling

> 1 egg
> 1 pound lean ground beef
> 7-ounce can whole kernel corn with sweet
>   peppers, drained
> ½ cup soda cracker crumbs
> ½ cup chili sauce
> 2 tablespoons sweet pepper flakes
> 1 tablespoon instant minced onion
> ½ teaspoon oregano
> 4 stuffed green olives, sliced
> 6 slices crisp, crumbled bacon, if desired

Topping

> 1 egg, slightly beaten
> 2 tablespoons milk
> ½ teaspoon salt
> ½ teaspoon dry mustard
> ½ teaspoon Worcestershire sauce
> 1 cup shredded Cheddar cheese

Slices of bacon and green olives garnish the cheese topping. You can call 'em to supper in less than an hour.

OVEN 425°   6 SERVINGS

Beat egg slightly in mixing bowl. Add ground beef, corn, cracker crumbs, chili sauce, sweet pepper flakes, onion and oregano. Mix well. Press meat mixture firmly into pastry-lined pie pan. Bake at 425° for 20 to 25 minutes. Spread Topping on Filling. Top with olives and bacon. Bake an additional 5 minutes or until cheese melts. Let stand 10 minutes before serving.

Topping: Combine egg and milk; add salt, dry mustard, Worcestershire sauce, and cheese.

Saturday Night Supper
Peek-A-View Stroganoff
Buttered Carrots
Tossed Salad with Thousand Island Dressing
Fresh or Canned Fruit
Crisp Cookie
Beverage

A batter that makes its own "crust" around the stroganoff. Do it in less than an hour.

Peek-A-View Stroganoff

    1-pound can beef stroganoff
    ¼ cup butter
    3 eggs
    1 cup Pillsbury's Best All Purpose Flour*
    1 teaspoon baking powder
    ½ teaspoon salt
    1 cup milk

<u>Golden Mushroom Sauce</u>

10½-ounce can condensed golden mushroom
    soup
    ½ cup dairy sour cream
    ¼ cup milk

OVEN 425°   6 SERVINGS

Place stroganoff in small saucepan over low heat while preparing batter. Melt butter in 2-quart casserole in oven. Beat eggs in small mixer bowl at high speed of mixer until light and fluffy. Add 2 tablespoons of the melted butter and remaining ingredients. Beat only until smooth. *Do not overbeat.* Pour batter into hot casserole. Immediately spoon stroganoff into center of batter. Bake at 425° for 25 to 30 minutes. Serve with Golden Mushroom Sauce.

<u>Golden Mushroom Sauce</u>: Combine ingredients in saucepan. Heat to boiling point, stirring constantly. Do not boil.

*For use with Pillsbury's Best Self-Rising Flour, omit baking powder and salt.

Cornbread is the perfect topping for the chili-flavored filling. It's ready to go in about an hour.

Man-Cooked Meal

    1 pound lean ground beef
    ⅓ cup chopped onion
10¾-ounce can condensed tomato rice soup
    2 tablespoons chili sauce
    1½ teaspoons chili powder
    ½ teaspoon salt
    ¼ teaspoon garlic salt
    ⅛ teaspoon pepper
    1 package Pillsbury Golden Corn Muffin
    Mix

OVEN 425°   5 SERVINGS

Combine ground beef and onion in 9-inch square baking pan. Bake at 425° for 20 minutes. Drain. Stir in soup, chili sauce, chili powder, salt, garlic salt and pepper. Spread evenly in bottom of pan. Prepare corn muffin mix as directed on package. Pour over meat mixture. Bake at 425° for 30 to 35 minutes.

Flavorful meatballs combine with Yorkshire pudding in one dish. Start an hour before the meal.

Yorkshire Burger

Meatballs
    I egg
    I pound lean ground beef
    I packet onion soup mix
    ¼ cup soda cracker crumbs
    2 tablespoons catsup
    ¼ teaspoon pepper

Topping
    2 eggs
    I cup milk
    I cup Pillsbury's Best All Purpose Flour*
    I teaspoon baking powder
    ½ teaspoon salt

Gravy
    I package Pillsbury Brown Gravy Mix
    ⅓ cup dairy sour cream

OVEN 425°   6 SERVINGS

Meatballs: Beat egg in bowl, add ground beef, onion soup mix, cracker crumbs, catsup and pepper. Blend well. Form into 16 meatballs. Place in a greased 8 or 9-inch square baking dish. Bake at 425° for 15 minutes.

Topping: Beat eggs and milk together in mixing bowl with a rotary beater. Add flour, baking powder and salt. Beat only until smooth. Pour batter over meatballs. Bake at 425° for 25 to 30 minutes or until golden brown. Serve with Gravy.

Gravy: Prepare gravy mix as directed on package. When thickened, blend in sour cream and heat I minute, do not boil.

*For use with Pillsbury's Best Self-Rising Flour, omit baking powder and salt.

MENU

Special Family Dinner
Chili Cheese Surprise
Broccoli with Lemon Butter
Toasted French Bread
Fruit Salad with Celery Seed Dressing
Date Bars
Beverage

Cheese Soup goes into this souffle-topped hot dish. Time this well at an hour and a quarter to serve immediately.

Chili Cheese Surprise

    I pound lean ground beef
    ¼ cup chopped onion
    6 tablespoons Pillsbury's Best All Purpose
      or Self-Rising Flour
    I teaspoon salt
    1½ teaspoons chili powder
  10¾-ounce can condensed Cheddar cheese
      soup
    ⅛ teaspoon paprika
    3 eggs, separated

OVEN 425°   5 TO 6 SERVINGS

Combine meat and onion in 1½-quart casserole. Bake uncovered at 425° for 20 minutes. Remove from oven; drain. Reduce oven temperature to 350°. Blend in 3 tablespoons flour, salt and I teaspoon chili powder. Combine soup, 3 tablespoons flour, ½ teaspoon chili powder and paprika in medium saucepan. Bring to a boil; boil I minute. Gradually blend hot mixture into slightly beaten egg yolks. Beat egg whites until stiff but not dry. Gradually fold hot cheese mixture into beaten egg whites. Pour over meat mixture in casserole. Place in pan with I-inch of water. Bake at 350° for 45 to 50 minutes or until a knife inserted in center of soufflé comes out clean. Serve immediately.

HIGH ALTITUDE ADJUSTMENT — 5,200 FEET. Increase baking time to 55 to 60 minutes.

23

24

Individual pastry foldovers with savory flavors.
You can whip them up in less than an hour.

Pieburgers

Crust

  2 cups Pillsbury's Best All Purpose Flour*
  1 teaspoon salt
  ⅔ cup shortening
  ½ cup shredded Cheddar cheese
  2 teaspoons caraway seed
  ½ cup milk
  1 teaspoon vinegar

Filling

  1 pound lean ground beef
  1 packet onion soup mix
  ⅓ cup chili sauce
  2 tablespoons flour
  2 tablespoons pickle relish
  ½ teaspoon salt

OVEN 400°   4 LARGE SERVINGS

Combine flour and salt. Cut in shortening. Stir in cheese and caraway seed. Add vinegar to milk. Stir into flour mixture until dough clings together. Divide in half on floured surface. Roll out half of dough to a 10-inch square. Cut into four 5-inch squares. Place on ungreased cookie sheet. Roll out remaining dough to an 11-inch square. Cut into four 5½-inch squares. Divide Filling mixture in fourths; shape each to within ½-inch of edge of pastry on cookie sheet. Moisten edge. Top with remaining square of pastry. Seal with fork. Prick top for escape of steam. Bake at 400° for 25 to 30 minutes.

Filling: Combine ground beef, onion soup mix, chili sauce, flour, pickle relish and salt.

*For use with Pillsbury's Best Self-Rising Flour, omit salt.

Cheese tucked in hamburger, sealed in refrigerated rolls and topped with sour cream. Eatable in about an hour.

Hidden Cheeseburgers

  1 pound lean ground beef
  1 egg
  ½ cup soda cracker crumbs
  1 teaspoon salt
  ½ teaspoon onion salt
  ¼ teaspoon pepper
  1 to 2 teaspoons prepared mustard
  6 sticks Cheddar cheese (3-inches long and
    ¼-inch thick)
  1 can Pillsbury Refrigerated Quick
    Parkerhouse Dinner Rolls
  ¼ cup dairy sour cream
    Garlic Salt
    Paprika

OVEN 350°   6 SERVINGS

Combine ground beef, egg, cracker crumbs, salt, onion salt and pepper in mixing bowl. Shape into 6 equal portions, 4-inches long. Make deep indentation down center of each. Spread with a little mustard. Place cheese stick in each. Bring meat around to seal cheese.

Open can; separate dough into 12 rolls. Press 1 unfolded Parkerhouse roll buttered side up into an oblong shape 5-inches long. Place cheeseburger on roll. Press another unfolded roll to a 5-inch length. Place on cheeseburger butter side down. Moisten edges with water. Stretch and press to seal top of each roll to bottom crust. Repeat with remainder of meat and rolls. Place in ungreased 13x9-inch pan, 2-inches apart. Spread with sour cream; sprinkle with garlic salt and paprika. Bake at 350° for 30 to 35 minutes until golden brown. Remove from pan immediately. Serve hot.

A touch of curry in the slashed crust makes this meat loaf something special. Give yourself an hour and a quarter.

Chuck Wagon Loaf

　　2 cups Pilllsbury's Best All Purpose Flour*
　　I tablespoon baking powder
.　½ teaspoon salt
　　½ teaspoon curry powder
　　½ cup water
　　¼ cup cooking oil
　　2 tablespoons catsup
　　　Milk
　　　Sesame seed

Filling
　　I pound lean ground beef
　　4-ounce can mushroom stems and pieces,
　　　drained
10¾-ounce can condensed Cheddar cheese
　　　soup
　　3 tablespoons flour
　　2 tablespoons instant minced onion
　　I teaspoon seasoned salt
　　½ teaspoon salt
　　¼ teaspoon poultry seasoning, if desired

Sauce
　　⅓ cup milk
　　I tablespoon catsup

OVEN 375°　　　　　　6 TO 8 SERVINGS

Combine flour, baking powder, salt and curry powder in mixing bowl. Combine water, oil and catsup. Add to dry ingredients all at once, stirring until dough clings together. Knead lightly on floured surface 8 times. Roll out to a 12x9-inch rectangle. Place Filling in row down center of rectangle. Bring each edge over and seal. Place seam-side down on ungreased cookie sheet. With knife make diagonal slashes 1½-inches apart through crust just to Filling. Brush with milk; sprinkle with sesame seed. Bake at 375° for 40 to 45 minutes. Cut in slices; serve with Sauce.

Filling: Combine ground beef, mushrooms, ½ cup cheese soup, flour, onion, seasoned salt, salt and poultry seasoning in mixing bowl.

Sauce: Blend milk and catsup with remainder of cheese soup. Heat to boiling.

*For use with Pillsbury's Best Self-Rising Flour, omit baking powder and salt in the Crust.

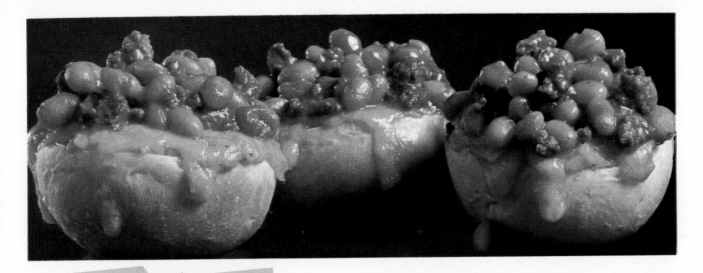

MENU

After The Game Supper
Hey Gang Snack Buns*
Potato Salad
Gelatin Fruit Salad
Relish Tray
Chocolate Cake
Beverage

*Prepare buns with cheese mixture and hamburger-bun mixture ahead. Heat bean mixture and pop bun under broiler just before serving.

Everything teenagers love. Make buns ahead for thirty minute assembly when served.

Hey Gang Snack Buns

    I package active dry yeast
    ¼ cup warm water
    I cup milk, scalded
    2 tablespoons sugar
    2 tablespoons cooking oil
    I teaspoon salt
    I egg
    3½ to 4 cups Pillsbury's Best All Purpose
        Flour*

Cheese Spread

    3 cups shredded cheese
    3 tablespoons finely chopped onion
    10¾-ounce can condensed tomato soup
    ½ teaspoon salt
    ⅛ teaspoon pepper

Hamburger-Bean Filling

    I pound lean ground beef
    2 (I-pound) cans pork and beans
    6-ounce can tomato paste
    2 tablespoons brown sugar
    2 tablespoons molasses
    I teaspoon salt
    I teaspoon dry mustard
    I teaspoon chili powder

OVEN 400°   16 ROLLS

Dissolve yeast in warm water. Combine milk, sugar, oil and salt. Add egg and half of flour to milk mixture. Beat until smooth. Stir in yeast. Gradually stir in remaining flour until a stiff dough forms. Cover. Let rise in warm place until doubled in size, I to I½ hours. Divide dough into 16 pieces. Shape each to make a bun and place on greased cookie sheet. Cover. Let rise in warm place until doubled in size. Bake at 400° for 12 to 15 minutes. Cool. Split buns. Spread halves with Cheese Spread. Place under broiler for 3 to 5 minutes until bubbly. Spoon Hamburger-Bean Filling over the rolls.

Cheese Spread: Combine cheese, onion, ½ can tomato soup, salt and pepper.

Hamburger-Bean Filling: Brown ground beef in skillet; drain. Stir in pork and beans, tomato paste, brown sugar, molasses, salt, dry mustard, chili powder and remainder of tomato soup. Simmer 10 minutes. Serve hot.

Tip: For quick snack buns, use hamburger buns.

*For use with Pillsbury's Best Self-Rising Flour, omit salt in rolls.

HIGH ALTITUDE ADJUSTMENT — 5,200 FEET.
During first rising time, decrease rising time from I½ hours to I hour.

MENU

Mid-Week Dinner
- Baked-In Beefburger
- Scalloped Potatoes
- French-Cut Green Beans
- Relish Tray
- Orange Sherbet
- Beverage

Casseroles and main dish meals are the perfect answer for busy homemakers and timesaving hostesses.

For added flavor to a company main dish try mushrooms, canned or fresh.

Surprise the family with a biscuit crusted meat loaf. Get an hour and a half start on dinner-time.

Baked-In Beefburger

*2 cups Pillsbury's Best All Purpose Flour**
1 tablespoon baking powder
½ teaspoon salt
¼ teaspoon sage, if desired
¼ teaspoon marjoram, if desired
⅓ cup water
⅓ cup cooking oil
8-ounce can tomato sauce
Milk
Celery seed, if desired

Filling

1 pound lean ground beef
1 teaspoon salt
½ cup soda cracker crumbs
2 tablespoons instant minced onion
1 egg

OVEN 375° — 6 TO 8 SERVINGS

Combine flour, baking powder, salt, sage and marjoram in mixing bowl. Combine water, cooking oil and ⅓ cup tomato sauce. Add to dry ingredients all at once, stirring until dough clings together. Knead lightly on floured surface 8 times. Roll out to a 15x8-inch rectangle. Spread Filling on dough to within ½-inch of 8-inch ends. Roll as for jelly roll starting with 8-inch end. Seal. Place seam-side down in greased 9x5-inch loaf pan or cookie sheet. With scissors or sharp knife make 8 slashes down ⅓ through loaf. Brush with milk; sprinkle with celery seed. Bake at 375° for 55 to 60 minutes. Let stand 10 minutes. Turn out of pan onto serving platter. Cut in slices to serve.

Filling: Combine ground beef, salt, cracker crumbs, onion, egg and remaining ⅔ cup tomato sauce.

*For use with Pillsbury's Best Self-Rising Flour, omit baking powder and salt.

Even the crust is flavorful and pink in this easy-ingredients pizza. Only forty-five minutes from start to finish.

American Piece-A-Pie

    2 cups Pillsbury's Best All Purpose Flour*
 1½ teaspoons baking powder
  ½ teaspoon salt
  ½ teaspoon chili powder
  ¼ cup shortening
  ½ cup milk
    8-ounce can tomato sauce
      Cooking oil
    2 cups shredded American cheese

Filling
  ½ pound lean ground beef
  ¼ cup chopped onion
    2 tablespoons flour
  ½ teaspoon salt
  ¼ teaspoon chili powder
  ⅛ teaspoon pepper

OVEN 450°   6 SERVINGS

Combine flour, baking powder, salt and chili powder in large mixing bowl. Cut in shortening. Add milk and ¼ cup tomato sauce. Stir until dough clings together. Knead 12 times on floured surface. Pat or roll out on ungreased cookie sheet to within ½-inch of edge. Flute edge. Brush with oil. Spread with Filling. Sprinkle with cheese. Bake at 450° for 10 to 15 minutes. Serve hot.

Filling: Combine ground beef, onion, flour, salt, chili powder, pepper and remaining tomato sauce.

Tip: Pillsbury Refrigerated Seasoned Pizza Dough and Pizza Sauce may be used for the crust and the tomato sauce used in the Filling. Stretch dough to a 14x11-inch rectangle. Flute to form standing rim.

*For use with Pillsbury's Best Self-Rising Flour, omit baking powder and salt.

Cheddar cheese soup and fresh tomatoes make this an out-of-the-ordinary pizza. It's out of the oven in less than an hour.

Cheeza Soupreme

 1¼ cups Pillsbury's Best All Purpose Flour*
 10¾-ounce can condensed Cheddar cheese
      soup
  ⅓ cup shortening
  ¼ teaspoon salt
    2 medium tomatoes, sliced
    1 tablespoon water
    4 stuffed green olives, sliced

Filling
    1 egg, slightly beaten
 1½ pounds lean ground chuck
  ¼ cup flour
  ¼ cup catsup
 1½ teaspoons seasoned salt
 1½ teaspoons Italian Seasoning
    1 teaspoon instant minced onion
  ½ teaspoon salt
  ½ teaspoon pepper

OVEN 425°   6 TO 8 SERVINGS

Combine flour, ⅓ cup soup, shortening and salt in small mixer bowl. Mix at lowest speed of mixer until dough begins to form, 15 to 30 seconds. Shape into a ball; flatten. Press evenly into 12-inch pizza pan. Flute edge as desired. Press Filling evenly over bottom of crust. Arrange tomato slices on top of Filling. Bake at 425° for 25 minutes. Remove from oven. Stir water into remainder of soup. Top each tomato slice with ½ teaspoon cheese sauce and an olive slice. Spoon remainder of cheese sauce around edge of meat. Bake 5 minutes longer or until cheese just starts to melt.

Filling: Combine ingredients in mixing bowl. Blend thoroughly.

No ordinary pizza; the shape is borrowed from coffee cakes. Pretty and original . . . made in about an hour.

Pizza Loaf

1 package Pillsbury Refrigerated Seasoned
  Pizza Dough and Pizza Sauce
1 pound lean ground beef
¼ cup chopped onion
4-ounce can mushroom stems and pieces,
  drained
2 tablespoons flour
1 tablespoon sweet pepper flakes
1 teaspoon paprika
¼ teaspoon leaf oregano
⅛ teaspoon pepper
½ cup chopped black olives, if desired
1 cup shredded Cheddar cheese
  Milk
  Sesame seed

Sauce
10¾-ounce can condensed tomato soup
1 cup shredded Cheddar cheese
½ teaspoon dry mustard
1 teaspoon Worcestershire sauce

OVEN 400°   6 TO 8 SERVINGS

Combine refrigerated pizza sauce, ground beef, onion, mushrooms, flour, sweet pepper flakes, paprika, oregano and pepper in skillet. Cook over medium heat 15 minutes. Remove from heat and stir in olives. Cool for 10 minutes.

Open can of pizza dough; unroll and place seasoned side up on a greased cookie sheet. Stretch dough to a 14x11-inch rectangle.

1. Place meat mixture down center third of dough.

2. Make diagonal cuts 2-inches apart on each side.

3. Fold strips over Filling, crossing in center.

4. Sprinkle with sesame seeds.

Place meat mixture down center third of dough to within 2-inches of ends. Sprinkle with Cheddar cheese. Make diagonal cuts 2-inches apart, on each side of rectangle just to edge of Filling. Fold ends over Filling. Then fold strips over Filling alternating sides and crossing in center. Brush with milk and sprinkle with sesame seed. Bake at 400° for 15 to 20 minutes or until golden brown. Serve as is or with Sauce.

Sauce: Combine tomato soup, shredded cheese, dry mustard and Worcestershire sauce in a saucepan. Heat over low heat until cheese is melted and mixture is smooth. Serve hot.

Golden Nugget Meatballs

Cheese is worked into the pastry for these individual burger pies. Prepare and bake in about an hour.

Cheese-Burger Buns

    I pound lean ground beef
    I packet onion soup mix
    I egg
    I tablespoon milk
      Dash of hot pepper sauce
    I cup Pillsbury's Best All Purpose or
      Self-Rising Flour
    ½ teaspoon paprika
    ¼ cup shortening
    6-ounce roll process cheese food, room
      temperature

OVEN 350°   6 SERVINGS

Combine ground beef, onion soup mix, egg, milk and hot pepper sauce. Divide into 6 equal portions; form each into a patty. Set aside. Combine flour, paprika, shortening and cheese food in small mixer bowl. Mix at lowest speed of mixer until dough begins to form, 15 to 30 seconds. Shape into a ball. Divide into 12 equal portions. Press 6 portions into 5-inch circles on greased cookie sheet. Top each with meat patty. On well-floured surface roll out each of the remaining 6 portions to 5-inch circles. Place over meat; press bottom edge to seal. Bake at 350° for 20 to 25 minutes until golden brown.

There are treasures within treasures in these sealed and seeded rounds of biscuit. Ready, gang, in about an hour.

Golden Nugget Meatballs

    I pound lean ground beef
    ½ cup dry bread crumbs or soda cracker
      crumbs
    ¼ cup catsup
    I teaspoon salt
    I teaspoon Worcestershire sauce
    ½ teaspoon onion salt
    5 (1½-inches square x ¼-inch thick)
      pieces of cheese
    I can Pillsbury Refrigerated Hungry Jack
      Flaky or Flaky Buttermilk Biscuits
      Milk
      Poppy seed
      Sesame seed

OVEN 375°   5 SERVINGS

Combine ground beef, bread crumbs, catsup, salt, Worcestershire sauce and onion salt in mixing bowl. Divide into 10 equal portions. Flatten each to a 4-inch circle on waxed paper or plastic wrap. Place a piece of cheese in center of 5 patties. Place remaining 5 patties on top of cheese. Pinch edges together well to seal in cheese. Smooth edges to make 4-inch patties.

Open can; separate dough into 10 biscuits. On ungreased cookie sheet pat 5 of the biscuits to make 5-inch circles. Place a burger on top of each; moisten edges with milk. Press out remaining biscuits to 5-inch circles. Stretch over burger and seal to bottom crust. Pinch together well to seal. Brush with milk and sprinkle with poppy seed or sesame seed. Bake at 375° for 25 to 30 minutes. Remove from cookie sheet immediately. Allow to cool 10 minutes before eating.

Tip: Make patties ahead, cover and refrigerate until ready to place inside biscuit and bake.

Prepare bread crumbs from leftover bread crusts and slices and have a ready supply in the refrigerator.

The Loveliest Luncheons

• The perfect luncheon entrée is attractive, distinctively good-tasting and, to all appearances, easy-on-the-hostess. The recipes in this section score well on all these counts, and they run the gamut from simple "Tun-au-Gratin" to the exquisite "Oriental Shrimp Sandwich Roll" that challenges your creativity. A word to the wise hostess: Plan your menu and table to the last detail; do everything possible ahead of time; relax and enjoy your company. Leave them murmuring, "How does she do it so easily?"

Finally! A soufflé that won't leave you flat, because it starts with cheese sauce. Time it tightly so you serve it right from the oven in about an hour and fifteen minutes.

Inflation Soufflé

6 tablespoons butter
⅔ cup Pillsbury's Best All Purpose Flour*
1 teaspoon salt
¼ teaspoon dry mustard
1½ cups milk
1½ cups shredded Cheddar cheese
½ teaspoon Worcestershire sauce
6 eggs, separated

OVEN 350°   6 TO 8 SERVINGS

Melt butter in large saucepan. Blend in flour, salt and mustard. Cook until bubbly. Gradually add milk. Cook over medium heat, stirring constantly, until very thick. Add cheese and Worcestershire sauce stirring until cheese melts. Remove from heat. Blend in egg yolks, one at a time, beating well after each. Beat egg whites until stiff but not dry. Fold into cheese mixture. Pour into ungreased 1½-quart casserole or soufflé dish. Set in pan containing 1-inch of hot water. Bake at 350° for 55 to 60 minutes until a knife inserted near the center comes out clean. Serve immediately.

Tip: For 3 to 4 servings, use half the recipe. Bake in 1-quart casserole for 40 to 45 minutes.

*For use with Pillsbury's Best Self-Rising Flour, omit salt.

HIGH ALTITUDE ADJUSTMENT — 5,200 FEET.
Bake at 350° for 65 to 70 minutes.

Sour cream and Parmesan cheese give extra ordinary flavor to this super soufflé. Give yourself an hour and three-quarters — before the moment you bring it grandly to the table.

Elegant Cheese Puff

2 cups soft bread cubes, without crusts
1 cup dairy sour cream
1/3 cup grated Parmesan cheese
1 teaspoon chopped chives
1/2 teaspoon salt
1/16 teaspoon cayenne pepper
4 eggs, separated

OVEN 350°   4 TO 6 SERVINGS

Combine soft bread cubes, sour cream, Parmesan cheese, chives, salt, cayenne pepper and egg yolks in large mixing bowl. Cover and let stand 30 minutes. Beat egg whites until stiff but not dry. Fold into egg yolk mixture. Pour into ungreased 1-quart casserole. Set in pan containing at least 1-inch hot water. Bake at 350° for 45 to 50 minutes until knife inserted in center comes out clean. Serve immediately.

Onion ring-arounds top this fancy tuna hot-dish made with simple ingredients. Whip it up easily in less than an hour.

Tun-Au-Gratin

3½-ounce can French fried onions
10½-ounce can condensed cream of
    mushroom soup
2 (6½-ounce) cans tuna fish, drained and
    flaked
10-ounce package frozen peas, thawed
1/3 cup milk
1/4 cup chopped pimiento
1 cup shredded American cheese

OVEN 375°   5 TO 6 SERVINGS

Combine onions (reserving 1 cup for topping), soup, tuna, peas, milk and pimiento in a 1½-quart casserole. Sprinkle with cheese. Cover and bake at 375° for 45 minutes. Top with remaining onions. Bake, uncovered, 3 to 5 minutes longer.

Tip: Casserole can be made ahead of time and refrigerated. Add 5 minutes to baking time.

To give your souffle a high crown or a "top-hat" use tip of spoon to trace circle in mixture 1-inch from edge and about 1-inch deep.

When planning the grocery list, allow 1/4 pound of cheese for each 1 cup shredded cheese.

For sophisticated palates, this unusual onion-ham-mushroom combination can star as a main dish, or, without the ham, play the role of elegant vegetable side-dish. One hour in the making.

Creamy Onion Delish

2 (10-ounce) packages frozen onions in
    cream sauce
3-ounce package cream cheese, cut in
    cubes
2 cups cubed cooked ham
4-ounce can mushroom stems and pieces,
    drained
1/4 teaspoon paprika
2 tablespoons butter
1/2 cup dry bread crumbs

OVEN 375°   6 TO 8 SERVINGS

Prepare onions as directed on package. Place in 1½-quart casserole. Add cream cheese and stir until blended. Stir in ham, mushrooms and paprika. Melt butter; blend in bread crumbs. Sprinkle over casserole. Bake at 375° for 25 to 30 minutes until golden brown and bubbly.

Tips: Prepare ahead, cover and refrigerate. Bake at 375° for 30 minutes.

For a vegetable side dish, omit ham; serve with baked ham, roast beef, turkey or chicken.

MENU

Bridge Luncheon
Hawaiian Tuna Puffs
Caramel Rolls
Relish Tray
Strawberry Parfaits
Beverage

Color this pink and green: Brussels sprouts and cubed luncheon meat, drenched in a chili-cheese sauce and nutty topping. Do ahead, or give yourself an hour and a quarter from start to serve.

Cook's Choice Casserole

10-ounce package frozen Brussels sprouts
1 cup cubed luncheon meat
4 hard-cooked eggs, sliced
1 cup shredded Cheddar cheese
2 tablespoons butter
2 tablespoons flour
1/2 teaspoon salt
1/8 teaspoon pepper
1 cup milk
1 tablespoon chili sauce
1/2 teaspoon horseradish

Topping
1/2 cup shredded Cheddar cheese
1/4 cup slivered almonds
2 tablespoons flour

OVEN 400°   4 TO 6 SERVINGS

Prepare Brussels sprouts as directed on package. Drain. Place in bottom of 1½-quart casserole. Top with luncheon meat, eggs and cheese. Melt butter in small saucepan. Blend in flour, salt and pepper. Gradually stir in milk. Cook over medium heat until mixture boils. Blend in chili sauce and horseradish. Pour over mixture in casserole. Sprinkle Topping over casserole. Bake at 400° for 25 to 30 minutes.

Topping: Combine cheese, almonds and flour.

Tip: Prepare ahead, cover and refrigerate. Bake at 400° for 35 to 40 minutes.

Served chilled, these soy flavored cream puffs filled with a crunchy pineapple-tuna mixture will wow your bridge club. Do ahead and easy, too.

Hawaiian Tuna Puffs

1 cup water
1/2 cup butter
1 tablespoon soy sauce
1 cup Pillsbury's Best All Purpose Flour*
1/4 teaspoon salt
4 eggs

Filling
8-ounce can crushed pineapple drained, reserving juice
2 (3-ounce) packages cream cheese, softened
1/2 cup chopped green pepper
2 tablespoons finely chopped onion
1/2 teaspoon paprika
2 teaspoons soy sauce
1 cup chopped celery
2 (6½-ounce) cans tuna, drained
5-ounce can water chestnuts, drained and chopped

OVEN 400°   12 SERVINGS

Bring water, butter and soy sauce to boil in medium saucepan. Add flour and salt all at once. Stir over medium heat until mixture leaves sides of pan, about 1 minute. Remove from heat. Blend in eggs, one at a time, beating vigorously after each until mixture is smooth and glossy. Drop by rounded tablespoonfuls onto greased cookie sheet. Bake at 400° for 45 to 50 minutes until golden brown and dry. Remove from cookie sheet immediately. Cool. Split and fill with chilled Filling just before serving.

Filling: Drain pineapple, reserving liquid. Blend together cream cheese, green pepper, onion and paprika until creamy. Blend in 1/4 cup pineapple juice and soy sauce. Add celery, pineapple, tuna and water chestnuts. Mix just to blend. Chill.

Tip: For hors d' oeuvres, drop dough by teaspoonfuls onto greased cookie sheet. Bake at 400° for 25 to 30 minutes. Cool. Split and fill just before serving. Makes 4 dozen.

*For use with Pillsbury's Best Self-Rising Flour, omit salt.

Individual savory puffs are split and filled with chilled chicken salad. A do-ahead entrée that lets you enjoy your own party. They make exquisite hors d' oeuvres too.

Onion Corn Puffs

  1 cup water
  ½ cup shortening
  ¾ cup Pillsbury's Best All Purpose or Self-Rising Flour
  ¼ cup corn meal
  1 packet onion soup mix
  4 eggs

Chicken Salad Filling

  3 cups cubed cooked chicken
  1 cup chopped celery
  1 cup shredded carrots
  ½ cup mayonnaise
  ¼ cup chopped pimiento
  ¼ cup chopped green pepper
  2 tablespoons lemon juice
  ½ teaspoon onion salt
  ⅛ teaspoon paprika

OVEN 375°   8 SERVINGS

Combine water and shortening in saucepan. Bring to boil. Add flour, corn meal and onion soup mix all at once. Cook and stir over medium heat until mixture leaves sides of pan. Remove from heat. Add eggs, one at a time, beating vigorously after each. Drop rounded tablespoonfuls onto greased cookie sheet. Bake at 375° for 40 to 45 minutes until deep golden brown. Remove from sheet immediately. Cool. Split and fill with chilled Chicken Salad Filling just before serving.

Chicken Salad Filling: Combine all ingredients. Chill.

Tip: For hors d' oeuvres, drop dough by teaspoonfuls onto greased cookie sheet. Bake at 375° for 25 to 30 minutes. Cool. Split and fill just before serving. Makes 4 dozen.

Creamy chicken and ham served in tender cream puffs. Give yourself an hour and a quarter to prepare this.

Luncheon Chicken Puffs

  1 cup water
  ½ cup shortening
  1 teaspoon dry mustard
  ½ teaspoon instant minced onion
  1 cup Pillsbury's Best All Purpose Flour*
  ¼ teaspoon salt
  3 eggs

Sauce

  2 tablespoons butter
  2 tablespoons flour
  1 cup milk
  ¼ teaspoon salt
  ⅛ teaspoon paprika
  1 cup cubed cooked chicken
  1 cup cubed cooked ham
  1 tablespoon dried parsley flakes

OVEN 400°   6 TO 8 SERVINGS

Combine water, shortening, mustard and onion in saucepan. Bring to boil. Add flour and salt all at once. Cook and stir over medium heat until mixture leaves sides of pan. Remove from heat. Add eggs, one at a time, beating vigorously after each. Drop rounded tablespoonfuls onto greased cookie sheet. Bake at 400° for 40 to 45 minutes until golden brown. Serve warm with Sauce.

Sauce: Melt butter in saucepan over medium heat; blend in flour until bubbly. Gradually stir in milk, salt and paprika. Cook over medium heat until mixture boils. Boil 1 minute. Stir in chicken, ham and parsley. Heat thoroughly.

Tips: If desired, use all chicken or all ham in Sauce.

To reheat puffs, place on cookie sheet in 350° oven for 10 to 15 minutes.

*For use with Pillsbury's Best Self-Rising Flour, omit salt.

MENU

Weekend Brunch
  Cheese Ham Wheels and Sweet Rolls
  Scrambled Eggs
  Broiled Grapefruit Halves
  Coffee

Beautiful pinwheels sprinkled with seeds. This yeast-dough recipe may be made ahead and reheated. Otherwise, give yourself three hours or more, including rising.

Cheese Ham Wheels

I package active dry yeast
¼ cup warm water
I tablespoon sugar
I tablespoon shortening
I teaspoon salt
½ cup milk, scalded
I egg
2½ to 3 cups Pillsbury's Best All Purpose Flour*
5 slices (4-ounces) American or Cheddar cheese
10 slices (8-ounces) boiled ham
  Milk
  Sesame or poppy seed

Soften yeast in warm water. Combine sugar, shortening, salt and milk in mixing bowl. Cool to lukewarm. Stir in egg and softened yeast. Gradually add flour to form a stiff dough, beating well after each addition. Cover. Let rise in warm place until light and doubled in size, about 1½ hours. Roll out dough on floured surface to an 8x20-inch rectangle. Cut into ten 4-inch squares. Place on greased cookie sheet. Cut cheese into 1½-inch squares. Top each square of dough with a square of cheese, then a ham slice and then another square of cheese. Cut with kitchen shears or sharp knife diagonally through layers of dough, ham and cheese from each corner to within ½-inch of center. Fold alternate points to center, overlapping and pinching gently to seal. Fasten with toothpick. Brush with milk. Sprinkle with sesame or poppy seed. Cover. Let rise until light and doubled in size, about 30 minutes. Bake at 400° for 15 to 18 minutes.

Tips: For dough, use 1 package Pillsbury Hot Roll Mix preparing as directed on package. Bake at 375° for 15 to 18 minutes.

Make ahead, then reheat by wrapping in foil and placing in 350° oven for 20 minutes.

*For use with Pillsbury's Best Self-Rising Flour, omit salt.

HIGH ALTITUDE ADJUSTMENT — 5,200 FEET. During first rising time, decrease rising time from 1½ hours to 1 hour.

1. Top dough with cheese, then ham.

2. Cut diagonally to within ½-inch of center.

3. Fold alternate points to center.

4. Sprinkle with poppy seeds.

41

Shoestring potatoes give the texture to the tuna filling that goes into these flavorful cream puffs. A cool and clever meal, that can be prepared in advance.

Filled Parmesan Puffs

    1 cup water
    ½ cup shortening
    1 cup Pillsbury's Best All Purpose Flour*
    ¼ teaspoon salt
    4 eggs
    ½ cup grated Parmesan cheese
    1 tablespoon corn meal
    ⅛ teaspoon cayenne pepper

Tuna Filling

    2 (6½-ounce) cans tuna
    1 cup chopped celery
    1 cup dairy sour cream
    ½ cup chopped stuffed green olives
    2 tablespoons finely chopped onion
    2 tablespoons pickle relish
    1 tablespoon lemon juice
    ¼ teaspoon salt
    ¼ teaspoon paprika
    1¾-ounce can (1½ cups) shoestring potatoes

OVEN 400°   8 SERVINGS

Combine water and shortening in saucepan. Bring to boil. Add flour and salt all at once. Cook and stir over medium heat until mixture leaves sides of pan. Remove from heat. Add eggs, one at a time, beating vigorously after each. Combine Parmesan cheese, corn meal and cayenne pepper. Drop dough by rounded tablespoonfuls into cheese mixture; roll to coat. Place on greased cookie sheet. Bake at 400° for 40 to 45 minutes until golden brown. Cool. Split and fill with Tuna Filling just before serving.

Tuna Filling: Combine tuna, celery, sour cream, olives, onion, relish, lemon juice, salt and paprika. Chill. Stir in shoestring potatoes just before filling puffs.

Tips: If puffs become soft, place on cookie sheet at 350° for 5 minutes. Cool.

For hors d' oeuvres, drop dough by teaspoonfuls. Bake at 400° for 25 to 30 minutes. Makes 4 dozen.

*For use with Pillsbury's Best Self-Rising Flour, omit salt.

Elegant shrimp salad fills these light airy cream puffs. You probably have all the ingredients right on your shelf. Make it several hours early and chill.

Shrimp Salad Puffs

    1 cup water
    ½ cup butter
    ¼ teaspoon hot pepper sauce
    1 cup Pillsbury's Best All Purpose Flour*
    ½ teaspoon salt
    4 eggs

Shrimp Filling

    2 cups cooked small shrimp
    1 cup chopped celery
    ¼ cup chopped ripe olives
    4 hard-cooked eggs, chopped
    ¼ cup mayonnaise or salad dressing
    2 tablespoons catsup
    1 tablespoon lemon juice
    ½ teaspoon salt
    1 teaspoon Worcestershire sauce

OVEN 400°   8 SERVINGS

Combine water, butter and hot pepper sauce in saucepan. Bring to boil. Add flour and salt all at once. Cook and stir over medium heat until mixture leaves sides of pan. Remove from heat. Add eggs, one at a time, beating vigorously after each. Drop by rounded tablespoonfuls onto greased cookie sheet. Bake at 400° for 40 to 45 minutes until golden brown. Cool. Split and fill with Shrimp Filling just before serving.

Shrimp Filling: Combine all ingredients. Chill until ready to serve.

Tips: For 4 puffs, cut recipe in half.

If puffs become soft, crisp by placing on cookie sheet in 350° oven for 5 minutes. Cool, then fill.

*For use with Pillsbury's Best Self-Rising Flour, omit salt.

MENU

Luncheon Buffet
  Oriental Celery Crunch
  Cranberry-Orange Gelatin Salad
  Relishes
  Hot Rolls
  Lemon Angel Pie
  Beverage

Under that cheese-nut pastry topping is celery and crunchy almonds in a rich cheese sauce. Makes a beautiful casserole in an hour.

Oriental Celery Crunch

¼ cup butter
3 cups sliced celery
¼ cup flour
1 teaspoon instant minced onion
½ teaspoon salt
1¾ cups milk
1 cup shredded Cheddar cheese
2 cups cubed cooked chicken

Topping

½ cup Pillsbury's Best All Purpose Flour*
¼ teaspoon salt
¼ cup butter
½ cup shredded Cheddar cheese
½ cup diced roasted almonds

OVEN 400°   4 TO 5 SERVINGS

Melt butter in a large skillet. Add celery and sauté, stirring occasionally, for 5 minutes. Stir in flour, onion and salt. Gradually add milk. Cook over medium heat, stirring constantly, until thickened. Blend in cheese and chicken. Pour into 1½-quart casserole. Sprinkle with Topping. Bake at 400° for 25 to 30 minutes until golden brown and bubbly.

Topping: Combine flour and salt. Cut in butter until particles are fine. Stir in cheese and almonds.

Tips: Prepare ahead. Cover and refrigerate. Bake at 400° for 30 minutes before serving.

For a vegetable side dish, omit chicken and use 4 cups sliced celery. Serve with chicken, ham or pork.

*For use with Pillsbury's Best Self-Rising Flour, omit salt.

Quick and easy-as-pie (well, it is a pie!). Pretty pink crabmeat, accented with green pepper, golden cheese. Less than an hour's time is required, for pastry shell and all.

Crabmeat Salad Bake

8-inch Baked Pastry Shell, see page 5

Crabmeat Salad Filling

7½-ounce can crabmeat, drained and flaked
1 cup chopped celery
1 cup shredded Cheddar cheese
¼ cup grated Parmesan cheese
¼ cup chopped green pepper
¼ cup mayonnaise
1 tablespoon lemon juice
1 teaspoon chopped chives
⅛ teaspoon hot pepper sauce
2 tablespoons dry bread crumbs
¼ cup slivered almonds

OVEN 350°   5 TO 6 SERVINGS

Combine crabmeat, celery, ¾ cup Cheddar cheese, Parmesan cheese, green pepper, mayonnaise, lemon juice, chives and hot pepper sauce in mixing bowl. Spoon into Baked Pastry Shell. Sprinkle with bread crumbs, remaining ¼ cup Cheddar cheese and slivered almonds. Bake at 350° for 15 to 20 minutes.

Quick refrigerated crescent roll crust makes the perfect setting for this smoky cheesy filling. Give yourself an hour and a half.

Pie A La Italiana

   1 can Pillsbury Refrigerated Quick Crescent Dinner Rolls
   8-ounce package Italian or Monterey Jack cheese, cut into ½-inch cubes
   12-ounce can luncheon meat, cut into ½-inch cubes or 12-ounce package smoked sausages, cut into ¼-inch slices
   ⅛ teaspoon salt
   ⅛ teaspoon pepper
   1 tablespoon grated Parmesan cheese
   2 eggs, slightly beaten

OVEN 325°   9-INCH PIE

Open can; unroll dough and separate into 8 triangles. Place 5 triangles in ungreased 9-inch pie pan pressing pieces together to form a crust. Reserve 3 triangles for top crust. Combine remaining ingredients in large mixing bowl. Pour into crust. Roll out each remaining triangle so longest side is 9-inches. Cut into ½-inch strips. Crisscross strips over filling to form a lattice top. Flute edge. Bake at 325° for 60 to 70 minutes or until knife inserted 2-inches from edge comes out clean. Do not overbake. Cool 10 minutes before cutting in wedges.

MENU

Saturday Luncheon Before A Game
   Pie A La Italiana
   Tossed Salad
   Assorted Rolls or Nut Breads
   Fruit Cup
   Coffee

Deviled ham sparks up this ring of corn bread topped with creamed chicken or eggs. Start forty-five minutes before you tell them lunch is served.

Hearty Ham Corncake

    1 cup Pillsbury's Best All Purpose Flour*
    1 cup corn meal
    2 teaspoons baking powder
    1 teaspoon salt
    ½ teaspoon soda
    1 cup buttermilk
    ¼ cup cooking oil
    2 eggs
    4½-ounce can deviled ham

Sauce

10½-ounce can condensed cream of chicken soup
    ½ cup milk
    1 tablespoon dried parsley flakes
    ¼ teaspoon salt
    ⅛ teaspoon pepper
    4 hard-cooked eggs, chopped or 2 cups cubed cooked chicken

OVEN 425°   6 SERVINGS

Combine flour, corn meal, baking powder, salt and soda in medium mixing bowl. Combine buttermilk, oil, eggs and deviled ham. Add to dry ingredients all at once, stirring only until moistened. Pour into greased 8 or 9-inch ring mold. Bake at 425° for 25 to 30 minutes or until it springs back when touched lightly. Unmold immediately onto serving plate. Cut into serving slices; top with Sauce.

Sauce: Combine soup, milk, parsley, salt, pepper and chopped egg *or* chicken. Heat.

*For use with Pillsbury's Best Self-Rising Flour, omit baking powder and salt.

Crab and spicy tomato sauce tucked in thin crepes that can be made ahead of time. Allow about thirty minutes to fix the crepes; forty-five minutes to fill and bake.

Cape Cod Crepes

    ½ cup Pillsbury's Best All Purpose Flour*
    ½ teaspoon salt
    2 eggs
    ⅔ cup milk
    1 tablespoon butter, melted
    ½ cup shredded Mozzarella cheese

Filling

    2 (8-ounce) cans tomato sauce
    ¾ teaspoon leaf oregano
    7½-ounce can crabmeat, drained and flaked
    1 tablespoon dried parsley flakes
    1 teaspoon instant minced onion
    4-ounce can mushroom stems and pieces, drained

OVEN 350°   4 SERVINGS

Combine flour and salt in mixing bowl. Add eggs, milk and butter. Mix until smooth. Heat a 6-inch skillet over medium heat; grease lightly. Pour batter, a scant ¼ cup at a time, into skillet. Tilt pan to make a 6-inch round thin pancake. Brown about 1 minute, turn and bake other side. Place 2 rounded tablespoonfuls of Filling on each crepe and roll up. Place in a 9-inch square baking dish. Pour remaining tomato sauce over crepes. Sprinkle with cheese. Bake uncovered at 350° for 20 minutes.

Filling: Combine tomato sauce and oregano. Reserve 1½ cups for topping. Add crabmeat, parsley, onion and mushrooms to remaining sauce.

Tip: Crepes can be made ahead and refrigerated.

*For use with Pillsbury's Best Self-Rising Flour, omit salt.

Creamy chicken filling wrapped in thin pancakes topped with tangy sour cream and golden melted cheese. Allow an hour and a quarter.

Filled Luncheon Pancakes

 4 eggs
 1⅓ cups milk
 ½ teaspoon salt
 1 cup Pillsbury's Best All Purpose Flour*
 1 cup shredded American cheese

Filling
 10½-ounce can condensed cream of chicken
  soup
 2 cups cubed cooked chicken
 ¼ cup chopped green pepper
 ¼ cup (2½-ounce can) mushroom stems
  and pieces, drained
 1 teaspoon instant minced onion

Topping
 ½ cup dairy sour cream

OVEN 375°   5 TO 6 SERVINGS

Combine eggs, milk and salt in medium mixing bowl with rotary beater. Add flour, beat until smooth. Heat a 7 or 8-inch skillet over medium high heat. (Be sure pan is hot before starting.) Grease lightly before each pancake. Pour batter, scant ¼ cup at a time, into skillet, tilting pan to spread evenly. When pancake is light brown and set; turn to brown other side. Spread scant ¼ cup Filling down center of each pancake; roll up. Place seam side down, in 12x8 or 13x9-inch baking dish. Spoon Topping over pancakes, spreading to cover. Sprinkle with cheese. Bake at 375° for 25 to 30 minutes.

Filling: Combine ¾ cup soup with the chicken, green pepper, mushrooms and onion.

Topping: Fold remainder of soup into sour cream.

Tips: Prepare ahead, cover and refrigerate. Bake at 375° for 30 to 35 minutes.

To prepare pancakes with mix; combine <u>4 eggs</u>, <u>1⅓ cups milk</u> <u>and 3 tablespoons oil</u> with rotary beater. Beat in 1 cup Pillsbury Extra Light Pancake Mix. Cook as directed.

*For use with Pillsbury's Best Self-Rising Flour, omit salt.

The prettiest party sandwich roll you ever made. Slice through shrimp, pineapple, pecans and water chestnuts, with giant olives for a core. Make it early and chill.

Oriental Shrimp Sandwich Roll

 5 eggs, separated
 ½ teaspoon cream of tartar
 2 tablespoons sugar
 ¼ cup water
 ¾ cup Pillsbury's Best All Purpose Flour*
 2 teaspoons baking powder
 1 teaspoon salt
 1 teaspoon dried parsley flakes
 10 large stuffed green olives
 5-ounce jar pasteurized cheese spread
  with pimiento, softened

Filling
 2 (4½-ounce) cans tiny shrimp, drained
 8-ounce package cream cheese, softened
 1 tablespoon lemon juice
 ½ cup chopped pecans
 1 cup drained crushed pineapple
 5-ounce can water chestnuts, drained and
  chopped
 ½ teaspoon salt

OVEN 400°   8 TO 10 SERVINGS

Grease bottom of 15x10-inch jelly roll pan, line with waxed paper and grease again. Beat egg whites with cream of tartar in large mixer bowl at high speed until frothy. Gradually add sugar; continue beating until stiff but not dry.

Combine egg yolks, water, flour, baking powder, salt and parsley flakes in small mixer bowl. Mix at low speed just until blended. By hand, fold egg yolk mixture into egg whites. Spread in pan. Bake at 400° for 10 to 12 minutes. Loosen edge; invert on wire rack; remove waxed paper.

Spread with Filling. Place olives along one 10-inch side. Starting with this side, roll up jelly roll fashion. Frost with cheese spread. Garnish with additional olives or chopped pecans, if desired. Refrigerate at least 2 hours.

Filling: Combine all ingredients in mixing bowl.

Tips: This can be made 24 hours in advance. Omit cheese spread. Wrap tightly in aluminum foil; refrigerate. Frost with cheese spread shortly before serving. Garnish if desired.

*For use with Pillsbury's Best Self-Rising Flour, omit baking powder and salt.

It's bacon and eggs, ham and cheese, baked on a crust and served in strips, a la quiche lorraine. Crust can be prepared ahead, the rest assembled and baked in less than an hour.

Brunch Pizza

1 cup Pillsbury's Best All Purpose Flour*
¼ teaspoon salt
1/16 teaspoon pepper
⅓ cup shortening
3 to 4 tablespoons water

Filling

½ pound sliced bacon
4 slices cooked ham
4-ounces sliced Swiss cheese
2 eggs, slightly beaten
¾ cup milk
¼ teaspoon salt

OVEN 425°   6 SERVINGS

Combine flour, salt and pepper in mixing bowl. Cut in shortening until particles are fine. Sprinkle water over mixture while stirring with fork until dough holds together. Form into a square. Flatten to ½-inch thickness; smooth edges. Roll out on a floured surface to a 10-inch square. Fit loosely into a 9-inch square pan.

Filling: Fry bacon until crisp. Drain on absorbent paper; crumble. Place ham slices on bottom of pastry-lined pan. Top with cheese slices, then bacon. Combine eggs, milk and salt; pour carefully over bacon. Bake at 425° for 18 to 20 minutes until lightly browned and set. Cool 5 to 10 minutes before cutting and serving.

Tip: If desired, prepare crust ahead, fit into pan, add ham, cheese and bacon. Cover tightly and refrigerate. Just before baking add egg and milk mixture. Increase baking time about 5 minutes.

*For use with Pillsbury's Best Self-Rising Flour, omit salt.

MENU

Ladies' Luncheon
Shrimp Scrolls
Broccoli Spears
Waldorf Salad
Pineapple Chiffon Pie
Beverage

Muffin-size shrimp roll-ups served with a pink shrimp sauce. So easy with ready-made refrigerated crescent dinner rolls and frozen soup. Fun to prepare, in about forty-five minutes.

Shrimp Scrolls

2 (4½-ounce) cans shrimp, drained
1 cup shredded Cheddar cheese
1 tablespoon dried parsley flakes
1 can Pillsbury Refrigerated Quick Crescent Dinner Rolls

Sauce

10-ounce can frozen cream of shrimp soup, thawed
½ cup milk
¼ cup catsup
1 teaspoon Worcestershire sauce

OVEN 350°   4 SERVINGS
                            (8 scrolls)

Chop shrimp into small pieces. Mix in cheese and parsley. Open can; unroll dough on lightly floured surface leaving dough together as one large rectangle. Press together to seal at perforations and seams to form a 12x7-inch rectangle. Sprinkle shrimp-cheese mixture over rectangle, reserving 1 cup for sauce. Starting with 12-inch side, roll up jelly roll fashion; seal edges. Cut into 8 pieces and place cut side down in greased muffin cups. Bake at 350° for 25 to 30 minutes until golden brown. Let stand in muffin cups 1 to 2 minutes before removing from pan. Serve hot with Sauce.

Sauce: Prepare soup as directed using ½ cup milk, catsup, Worcestershire sauce and adding reserved shrimp and cheese.

Winning Family Suppers

• Everyday meats need not be everyday dull, as proven by the creative recipes in this section. For salmon or sausage, for corned beef or franks, there is a new look, a bright new flavor, or a terrific topping that will make your family take appreciative notice of your efforts in the kitchen.

A savory mixture made top-of-the range. Notice the currants in the dumplings. Start three hours in advance and let it simmer and steep.

Beef Stew With Deauville Dumplings

    2 pounds stewing beef, cut in I-inch cubes
    2 tablespoons shortening
    4 cups hot water
    2 onions, sliced
    I bay leaf
    I tablespoon salt
    ¼ teaspoon pepper
    6 carrots, cut in I-inch strips
    6 potatoes, cut in quarters
    10-ounce package frozen peas
    ¼ cup flour
    ½ cup cold water
    I teaspoon bottled brown bouquet sauce,
        if desired

Dumplings

    1½ cups Pillsbury's Best All Purpose Flour*
    2 teaspoons baking powder
    ½ teaspoon salt
    ½ cup currants
    I egg, slightly beaten
    ½ cup milk
    2 tablespoons cooking oil
    I teaspoon instant minced onion

8 TO 10 SERVINGS

Brown beef in shortening in a Dutch oven or large skillet. Stir in hot water, sliced onions, bay leaf, salt and pepper. Cover; simmer for 1½ to 2 hours until meat is tender. Remove bay leaf. Add carrots and potatoes. Cover and cook 20 to 30 minutes until almost tender. Add peas. Combine flour and cold water. Add to hot stew, stirring until thickened. Heat to boiling. Add bouquet sauce, if desired. Top with Dumplings.

Dumplings: Combine flour, baking powder, salt and currants in mixing bowl. Add egg, milk, oil and onion. Mix only until moist. Drop 8 to 10 tablespoonfuls on top of stew. Cover. Steam 12 to 15 minutes. Do not remove cover during steaming.

*For use with Pillsbury's Best Self-Rising Flour, omit baking powder and salt.

A treat for chili-lovers. Allow two hours and forty-five minutes preparation time.

Mexicali Stew

    ½ cup Pillsbury's Best All Purpose or
        Self-Rising Flour
    3 teaspoons chili powder
    I teaspoon salt
    ¼ teaspoon pepper
    I pound stewing beef, cut in I-inch cubes
    3 tablespoons cooking oil
    I packet onion soup mix
    2 cups hot water
    15½-ounce can kidney beans, undrained
    12-ounce can whole kernel corn with sweet
        peppers, undrained

Biscuits

    I can Pillsbury Refrigerated Hungry Jack
        Flaky or Flaky Buttermilk Biscuits
    2 tablespoons milk
    ¼ cup corn meal

OVEN 425°   4 TO 6 SERVINGS

Combine ¼ cup flour, I teaspoon chili powder, salt and pepper in a 2-quart casserole. Add stew meat and coat with flour mixture. Add oil. Bake uncovered at 425° for 20 minutes. Remove from oven; decrease oven temperature to 300°. Add ¼ cup more flour, onion soup mix, 2 teaspoons chili powder and hot water. Mix well. Cover and bake at 300° for 1½ to 2 hours until meat is tender. Add kidney beans and corn. Return to oven for 15 minutes. Serve piping hot with Biscuits.

Biscuits: Open can, separate dough into 10 biscuits. Dip each biscuit in milk, then roll in corn meal. Place on an ungreased cookie sheet about 2-inches apart. Bake as directed on label.

Tip: I (I-pound) can Mexican Style Red Beans can be used in place of kidney beans; reduce chili powder to I teaspoon.

Dublin Stew With Dumplings

I pound pork shoulder, cut in I-inch cubes
⅓ cup Pillsbury's Best All Purpose or
    Self-Rising Flour
2 cups carrots, cut in I-inch pieces
½ cup chopped onion
½ cup chopped celery
I clove garlic, minced
2 cups water
1½ teaspoons salt
I teaspoon bottled brown bouquet sauce
3 beef bouillon cubes
10-ounce package frozen mixed vegetables,
    thawed

Dumplings
I cup Pillsbury's Best All Purpose Flour*
2 teaspoons sugar
1½ teaspoons baking powder
½ teaspoon salt
¼ teaspoon dry mustard
I teaspoon caraway seed·
⅓ cup milk
I egg
2 tablespoons cooking oil

Tiny vegetables and bite-size pork bobbing in savory seasoning, dumpling topped, ready in an hour and a half.

OVEN 400°   6 TO 8 SERVINGS

Combine pork shoulder and flour in 3-quart casserole. Bake uncovered at 400° for 20 minutes. Add carrots, onion, celery, garlic, water, salt, bouquet sauce and bouillon. Cover and bake at 400° for 40 minutes. Remove from oven. Stir in mixed vegetables. Drop Dumplings by tablespoonfuls onto hot stew; cover and bake at 400° for 25 minutes.

Dumplings: Combine flour, sugar, baking powder, salt, mustard and caraway seed in mixing bowl. Combine milk, egg and oil. Add to dry ingredients all at once, stirring only until moistened.

*For use with Pillsbury's Best Self-Rising Flour, omit baking powder and salt.

51

Saturday Night Supper
Ham 'N Corn Fritters
Fruit and Cottage Cheese on Lettuce Leaf
Lemon Sherbet
Beverage

Tasty appetizers or a terrific simple supper. Only thirty minutes to prepare.

Ham 'N Corn Fritters

1½ *cups Pillsbury's Best All Purpose Flour**
2 *teaspoons baking powder*
I *teaspoon salt*
I *teaspoon dry mustard*
½ *cup milk*
2 *tablespoons cooking oil*
2 *eggs*
1½ *cups chopped cooked ham*
I-*pound can whole kernel corn, drained*

Cheese Sauce
10½ *-ounce can condensed Cheddar cheese soup*
⅓ *cup milk*
¼ *teaspoon Worcestershire sauce*

6 SERVINGS

Combine flour, baking powder, salt and dry mustard in mixing bowl. Combine milk, oil and eggs. Add to dry ingredients along with ham and corn. Stir just until moistened.

Drop by tablespoonfuls into I to 2 inches hot fat (375°F) and fry on both sides until golden brown, 3 to 4 minutes. Serve hot with Cheese Sauce or maple syrup.

Cheese Sauce: Combine all ingredients in saucepan; heat.

Tips: For appetizers, drop batter by teaspoonfuls and fry 2 to 3 minutes. Serve hot on toothpicks with Cheese Sauce or favorite dip.

Use an electric frypan with I to 2 inches fat or oil for frying fritters. Set thermostat at 375°F.

**For use with Pillsbury's Best Self-Rising Flour, omit baking powder and salt.*

An easy version of the typical English pork pie. A make-ahead delight. Takes only one hour.

Pork and Tater Pie

9-inch Unbaked Pastry Shell, see page 5
I *pound pork sausage*
¼ *cup chopped onion*
10¼ *-ounce can frozen cream of potato soup, thawed*
½ *cup water*
10-*ounce package frozen mixed vegetables, thawed*
¼ *cup dry bread crumbs*
¼ *cup grated Parmesan cheese*

OVEN 425°   6 SERVINGS

Sauté sausage and onion in skillet until well browned. Drain off excess fat. Stir in soup, water and mixed vegetables. Cover and simmer 5 minutes. Pour into Unbaked Pastry Shell. Combine bread crumbs and Parmesan cheese. Sprinkle over top. Bake at 425° for 25 to 30 minutes until golden brown.

Tip: To make ahead, prepare as directed except for adding crumb topping. Just before baking, add crumb topping.

Round steak takes on new flavor dimensions with buttermilk and Swiss cheese crusty biscuit top. Give yourself two and a half hours.

Cheese-Steak Casserole

1½ pounds round steak, cut into ½-inch
    strips
¼ cup flour
½ teaspoon salt
⅛ teaspoon pepper
 1 packet onion soup mix
 4-ounce can mushroom stems and pieces,
    undrained
 1 cup water
½ cup buttermilk or sour milk
 4-ounces Swiss cheese, sliced

Drop Biscuits
 1 cup Pillsbury's Best All Purpose Flour*
1½ teaspoons baking powder
½ teaspoon soda
½ teaspoon salt
½ cup buttermilk or sour milk
 3 tablespoons cooking oil

OVEN 350°   6 SERVINGS

Place meat in 8 or 9-inch square baking dish. Sprinkle flour, salt and pepper over meat. Mix to coat meat with flour. Bake at 350° for 30 minutes. Remove from oven. Stir in onion soup mix, mushrooms and water. Cover and bake 1½ hours or until meat is tender. Remove from oven. Set oven temperature at 450°. Pour ½ cup buttermilk over top of meat. Place one layer of Swiss cheese slices over top; reserve remaining cheese slices. Drop Biscuits by tablespoonfuls onto meat mixture. Cut remaining cheese in small pieces; sprinkle over biscuits. Bake at 450° for 15 to 18 minutes.

Drop Biscuits: Combine flour, baking powder, soda and salt in mixing bowl. Combine buttermilk and oil. Add to dry ingredients all at once stirring until dry particles are moistened.

Tip: To sour milk, place 1 tablespoon vinegar or lemon juice in measuring cup; add milk to make 1 cup.

*For use with Pillsbury's Best Self-Rising Flour, omit baking powder and decrease salt to ¼ teaspoon in Drop Biscuits.

Be a left-over genius! Biscuits made with raisins and cinnamon give ham a new face in 60 minutes.

Ham 'N Biscuit Supper

 2 cups cubed cooked ham
 8-ounce can whole kernel corn, drained
10¼-ounce can frozen condensed cream of
    potato soup, thawed
 1 tablespoon dried celery flakes
 1 teaspoon sugar
 1 teaspoon instant minced onion
¼ teaspoon dry mustard
¼ cup milk

Drop Biscuits
 1 cup Pillsbury's Best All Purpose Flour*
 2 teaspoons baking powder
½ teaspoon salt
⅓ cup raisins
⅛ teaspoon cinnamon, if desired
¼ cup milk
 3 tablespoons cooking oil
 1 egg

OVEN 400°   4 TO 6 SERVINGS

In 2-quart casserole combine ham, corn, potato soup, celery flakes, sugar, onion, mustard and milk. Cover and bake at 400° for 30 minutes. Remove from oven. Drop Biscuits by tablespoonfuls on top of ham mixture. Bake at 400° for 15 to 18 minutes.

Drop Biscuits: Combine flour, baking powder and salt in mixing bowl. Add raisins and cinnamon. Combine milk, oil and egg; add to dry ingredients stirring only until moistened.

*For use with Pillsbury's Best Self-Rising Flour, omit baking powder and salt.

You'll love the looks of the spooned-on "lattice" top garnished with pimiento and parsley. Entire preparation should be only about an hour and a quarter.

Gaelic Corned Beef

  4 cups cabbage, shredded or chopped
10½-ounce can condensed cream of celery
    soup
  12-ounce can corned beef, crumbled
  ½ cup milk
   I teaspoon salt
  ½ teaspoon caraway seed
  ⅛ teaspoon pepper
    Parsley
    Pimiento

<u>Drop Biscuits</u>
  ¾ cup Pillsbury's Best All Purpose Flour*
  ¼ cup corn meal
 I½ teaspoons baking powder
  ½ teaspoon salt
  3 tablespoons milk
  3 tablespoons cooking oil
  I egg

OVEN 400°   6 SERVINGS

Combine cabbage, soup, corned beef, milk, salt, caraway seed and pepper in 2-quart casserole. Cover. Bake at 400° for 30 minutes. Remove from oven. Increase oven temperature to 425°. Drop Biscuits by teaspoonfuls in crisscross rows. Bake uncovered at 425° for I5 to 20 minutes until golden brown. Garnish top with sprigs of parsley and pieces of pimiento alternately between biscuits.

<u>Drop Biscuits:</u> Combine flour, corn meal, baking powder and salt in mixing bowl. Combine milk, oil and egg. Add to dry ingredients all at once, stirring only until dry ingredients are moistened.

*For use with Pillsbury's Best Self-Rising Flour, omit baking powder and salt.

Sausage spokes with spicy apple rings baked in your skillet like an upside-down cake. Ready for brunch in less than an hour.

Sausage Wheel

 14-ounce jar spiced apple rings, drained, reserving liquid
 8-ounce package brown 'n serve Sausages
 I egg, slightly beaten
 ½ cup cooking oil
 I cup quick-cooking rolled oats
 I cup Pillsbury's Best All Purpose Flour*
 ½ cup brown sugar, firmly packed
 I cup buttermilk or sour milk
 I teaspoon baking powder
 ½ teaspoon salt
 ½ teaspoon soda

Buttered Spicy Syrup
 I cup sugar
 2 tablespoons butter

OVEN 400°   6 SERVINGS

Drain apple rings; reserve liquid. Place sausages in a heavy 9 or 10-inch ovenproof skillet in a 400° oven for 15 to 20 minutes or until browned. Arrange sausages spoke-fashion in the greased skillet, placing one apple ring in center. Combine remaining ingredients in mixing bowl. Stir just until moistened. Drop about half of the batter by tablespoonfuls between sausages and over apple ring. Spread evenly. Arrange remaining apple rings over batter; spread with remaining batter. Bake at 400° for 20 to 25 minutes or until browned. Invert onto serving plate. Serve hot with syrup if desired.

Buttered Spicy Syrup: Add water to reserved apple ring liquid to make I cup. Combine with sugar in saucepan. Bring to a boil, stirring occasionally. Remove from heat. Stir in butter.

Tip: To protect skillet handle, cover with aluminum foil before placing in oven.

*For use with Pillsbury's Best Self-Rising Flour, omit baking powder, salt and soda.

The beloved Reuben sandwich, here in a quick casserole version that takes only fifty minutes to prepare and bake.

Reuben Casserole

 I-pound II-ounce can sauerkraut, drained
 2 medium tomatoes, sliced
 2 tablespoons Thousand Island Dressing
 2 (4-ounce) packages sliced corned beef, shredded
 2 cups (8-ounces) shredded Swiss cheese
 I can Pillsbury Refrigerated 6 Tenderflake Biscuits or Tenderflake Buttermilk Biscuits
 2 crisp rye crackers, crushed
 ¼ teaspoon caraway seed

OVEN 425°   6 TO 8 SERVINGS

Spread sauerkraut in bottom of 12x8-inch or 9-inch square baking dish. Top with tomato slices, dot with dressing. Cover with corned beef; sprinkle with cheese. Bake at 425° for 15 minutes. Remove casserole from oven. Open can; separate dough into 6 biscuits. Separate each biscuit into 3 layers; slightly overlap layers on casserole to form 2 rows on 12x8-inch casserole; 3 rows on 9-inch square baking dish. Sprinkle with crackers and caraway seed. Bake at 425° for 15 to 18 minutes, until biscuits are golden brown.

Tips: If desired, 6 crisp rye crackers, crushed and blended with 2 tablespoons butter and ¼ teaspoon caraway seed, may be sprinkled over the cheese instead of the biscuit topping. Garnish with parsley.

To shred corned beef, cut in thin strips with kitchen shears.

A fried bread, shaped like a pronto-pup with Cheddar cheese sticks inside. This yeast recipe should be started two and a half hours ahead.

Hot Cheese Pups

SKILLET 325°   16 ROLLS

    1 package active dry yeast
    ¼ cup warm water
    1 cup milk, scalded
    ¼ cup butter
    2 tablespoons sugar
    1½ teaspoons salt
    1 egg
    3½ to 4 cups Pillsbury's Best All Purpose
        Flour*
    1 pound Cheddar cheese or American
        cheese
        Onion powder or finely chopped onion
        Butter

Soften yeast in warm water. Combine milk, butter, sugar, salt and egg in mixing bowl. Cool to lukewarm. Add 1 cup flour; beat well. Stir in yeast. Add remainder of flour, stirring to form a stiff dough. Cover; let rise in warm place until light and doubled, about 1 hour. Roll out dough, half at a time, on floured surface to a 14x8-inch rectangle. Cut into eight 7x2-inch pieces. Cut cheese into sticks about 6-inches long and ½-inch thick. Place one in center of each piece of dough. Sprinkle each with onion powder or ½ teaspoon finely chopped onion. Bring edges to center; pinch

to seal. Seal ends. Place seam-side down on tray. Cover; let rise in warm place, about 30 minutes. Fry in heavily-buttered skillet on medium heat (325° to 350° F.) about 2 minutes on each side. Turn carefully to brown all sides. Add more butter as necessary. Serve hot.

Tips: For variety, add crumbled crisp bacon with cheese. Or, fill with frankfurters instead of cheese.

To reheat, place on ungreased cookie sheet. Place uncovered in 350° oven for 15 minutes.

*For use with Pillsbury's Best Self-Rising Flour, omit salt.

I. Bring edges of dough over cheese; pinch to seal.

2. Fry in heavily buttered skillet.

For added texture don't overlook onion, celery or water chestnuts as a nice addition to even your "every-day" casserole.

Sour cream and chives in the biscuit topping add the crowning touch. Usual preparation time is just about an hour.

Danish Salmon Supper

    10-ounce package frozen peas and carrots, thawed
   ½ cup chopped green pepper
10½-ounce can condensed cream of mushroom soup
    1-pound can salmon, drained and broken into large pieces
   ¼ cup mayonnaise
   2 tablespoons lemon juice

Biscuits

   1½ cups Pillsbury's Best All Purpose Flour*
   2 tablespoons chopped chives
   2 teaspoons baking powder
   ½ teaspoon salt
   ¼ teaspoon soda
   ¼ cup shortening
   ½ cup dairy sour cream
   ¼ cup water

OVEN 425°   5 TO 6 SERVINGS

Combine peas and carrots, green pepper, soup, salmon, salad dressing and lemon juice in a 9-inch square baking dish. Top with Biscuits. Bake at 425° for 25 to 30 minutes.

Biscuits: Combine flour, chives, baking powder, salt and soda. Cut in shortening until particles are fine. Add sour cream and water. Stir until dough clings together. Knead on lightly floured surface 10 times. Roll out on floured surface to ½-inch thickness. Cut into rounds with 2-inch cutter.

*For use with Pillsbury's Best Self-Rising Flour, add 2 tablespoons flour and omit baking powder and salt.

You've never had an egg salad sandwich quite like this. Hot egg salad baked inside flaky refrigerated biscuits. Pull them from the oven in about an hour.

Egg Salad Foldovers

   4 hard-cooked eggs, chopped
  ¼ cup finely chopped celery
  ¼ cup mayonnaise
   1 teaspoon prepared mustard
  ½ teaspoon instant minced onion
  ½ teaspoon salt
  ⅛ teaspoon pepper
   1 can Pillsbury Refrigerated Hungry Jack Flaky or Flaky Buttermilk Biscuits

OVEN 400°   4 SERVINGS

Combine all ingredients except biscuits. Open can; separate dough into 10 biscuits. Press biscuits into 5-inch circles on ungreased cookie sheet. Place rounded tablespoonful of filling on each. Fold over; moisten with water and seal edges. Bake at 400° for 15 to 18 minutes, until golden brown.

When buying canned salmon, remember "red salmon" will add a deep salmon color but is more expensive while "pink salmon" is less expensive but will add less color.

MENU

Family Supper
Simple Salmon Pie
Brussels Sprouts
Fruit Gelatin Salad
Apple Crisp
Beverage

Bound with a cream sauce, topped with crushed cereal or potato chips. This takes an hour and a quarter.

Simple Salmon Pie

9-inch Unbaked Pastry Shell, see page 5
   2 tablespoons butter
   3 tablespoons flour
   I cup milk
   I teaspoon salt
   ⅛ teaspoon pepper
   I-pound can salmon, drained and broken
     into large pieces
   ½ cup coarsely chopped pimiento
   8-ounce can peas, drained
   I egg

Topping
   2 tablespoons butter
   ½ cup corn flakes, coarsely crushed

OVEN 425°   6 SERVINGS

Melt butter in a medium saucepan. Blend in flour. Gradually add milk, stirring constantly; cook until thickened. Remove from heat. Add salt, pepper, salmon, pimiento, peas and egg. Turn into Unbaked Pastry Shell. Sprinkle with Topping. Bake at 425° for 25 to 30 minutes. Cool 10 minutes before serving.

Topping: Melt butter, add crushed cereal; mix.

Tips: Potato chips or any other crisp cereal can be used for Topping.

Two 9¼-ounce cans tuna, well drained, can be substituted for salmon.

They're hot from the oven and easy-made with refrigerated biscuits. A hit with the children, too. Ready in about an hour.

Gay Tuna Sandwiches

6½-ounce can tuna, drained
  2 hard-cooked eggs, chopped
1½ cups shredded Cheddar cheese
  ¼ cup chopped green pepper
  2 tablespoons sweet pickle relish
  2 tablespoons chopped pimiento
  I teaspoon lemon juice
  I can Pillsbury Refrigerated Hungry Jack
    Flaky or Flaky Buttermilk Biscuits

OVEN 375°   5 SERVINGS

Combine all ingredients except biscuits. Open can; separate into 10 biscuits. Press five biscuits into 5-inch circles on ungreased cookie sheet. Top each with ½ cup filling. Press remaining biscuits into 6-inch circles. Stretch each over filling and seal to bottom biscuits. Bake at 375° for 20 to 25 minutes until golden brown.

Creamed ham and succotash served in toast cups. A great last-minute supper, ready in forty-five minutes.

Succotash Supper

10-ounce package frozen succotash, partially
    thawed
⅔ cup boiling water
2 tablespoons finely chopped onion
2 tablespoons butter
2 tablespoons flour
1 cup milk
1 cup cubed cooked ham
2 tablespoons finely chopped pimiento
½ teaspoon salt
⅛ teaspoon pepper

<u>Toast Cups</u>

8 slices bread
6 tablespoons butter, melted

OVEN 375°   4 SERVINGS

Cook succotash in boiling water 3 to 4 minutes. Drain thoroughly. Sauté onion in butter in a medium saucepan until tender. Blend in flour, stirring until smooth. Add milk gradually; cook, stirring constantly, until thickened. Stir in succotash, ham, pimiento, salt and pepper. Bring to boil, cover, simmer for 10 minutes. Serve over Toast Cups or other shells.

<u>Toast Cups</u>: Trim crust from bread. Brush both sides of each slice with butter. Press each slice into a muffin cup. Bake at 375° for 8 to 10 minutes until golden brown.

MENU

Sunday Night Supper
Succotash Supper
Lettuce Wedges with French Dressing
Fruit
Beverage

Just before serving, add a colorful touch to your main dish with fresh parsley, pepper rings, watercress, pimiento strips, sliced olives or garnish with some ingredient used in the dish.

Shrimp 'N Dumpling Creole

10½-ounce can condensed tomato soup

    4-ounce can mushroom stems and pieces, drained

    4½-ounce can tiny shrimp, drained

    I onion, sliced

    ½ green pepper, thinly sliced

    ¼ cup water

    I teaspoon Worcestershire sauce

    ¼ teaspoon salt

Cheese Dumplings

    ¾ cup Pillsbury's Best All Purpose Flour*

    I teaspoon baking powder

    ½ teaspoon salt

    ½ cup cubed (½-inch squares) Cheddar cheese

    ⅓ cup milk

    I tablespoon cooking oil

This is like an oven-baked creole that is topped with cheesy dumplings. Make it in an hour from things on your pantry shelf.

OVEN 350°   4 TO 6 SERVINGS

Combine soup, mushrooms, shrimp, onion, green pepper, water, Worcestershire sauce and salt in 1½-quart casserole. Cover. Bake at 350° for I hour. Remove from oven. Drop Cheese Dumplings by rounded teaspoonfuls onto hot mixture. Cover and bake for 20 minutes.

Cheese Dumplings: Combine flour, baking powder and salt in mixing bowl. Stir in cheese cubes. Combine milk and oil; add to dry ingredients all at once; stirring only until moistened.

*For use with Pillsbury's Best Self-Rising Flour, omit baking powder and salt.

Emergency dinner from the pantry shelf. Start eating in forty minutes.

Tijuana Hash

¼ cup butter
3-ounce package cream cheese
¾ cup Pillsbury's Best All Purpose
   or Self-Rising Flour
15-ounce can corned beef hash
¼ cup chopped green pepper
¼ cup chili sauce
1 teaspoon chili powder
½ teaspoon onion powder
1 cup shredded Cheddar cheese

OVEN 425°   6 SERVINGS

Place butter and cream cheese in 9-inch pie pan. Place in oven to melt butter (cream cheese will not melt). Remove from oven. Add flour and mix until a dough forms. Press in bottom and sides of pie pan. Combine hash, green pepper, chili sauce, chili powder and onion powder. Spoon into pastry; sprinkle with cheese. Bake at 425° for 15 to 20 minutes until golden brown.

Scalloped potatoes become a main dish with salmon and eggs, steeped in a savory sauce. Allow yourself two hours to prepare it.

Seaside Supper

4 cups sliced raw potatoes
4 hard-cooked eggs, sliced
2 tablespoons dried parsley flakes
1-pound can salmon, drained and flaked
10½-ounce can condensed cream of
   mushroom soup
½ cup milk
½ teaspoon salt
½ teaspoon Worcestershire sauce
1/16 teaspoon cayenne pepper
1 cup crushed potato chips

OVEN 350°   5 TO 6 SERVINGS

Place half of potatoes in 2-quart casserole. Top with half of eggs, half of parsley and half of salmon. Repeat. Combine soup, milk, salt, Worcestershire sauce and cayenne pepper. Pour over ingredients in casserole. Cover. Bake at 350° for 1 hour. Remove cover; sprinkle with potato chips. Bake uncovered for 30 minutes or until potatoes are tender.

Creative corned beef hash topped with tempting corn bread. Allow yourself an hour to prepare.

Corn 'N Beef Bake

2 (15-ounce) cans corned beef hash
⅓ cup chili sauce
1 tablespoon dry onion flakes
3 tablespoons barbecue sauce

<u>Corn Bread Topping</u>
½ cup Pillsbury's Best All Purpose Flour*
½ cup corn meal
2 teaspoons sugar
1 teaspoon baking powder
½ teaspoon salt
½ cup milk
2 tablespoons cooking oil
1 egg, slightly beaten
12-ounce can whole kernel corn with sweet
   pepper, well drained

OVEN 425°   6 TO 8 SERVINGS

Combine hash, chili sauce, onion and barbecue sauce in a 2-quart casserole. Pour Corn Bread Topping over mixture, spreading to cover. Bake at 425° for 45 to 50 minutes.

<u>Corn Bread Topping</u>: Combine flour, corn meal, sugar, baking powder and salt in mixing bowl. Add milk, oil and egg; stir until smooth. Add corn; mix well.

*For use with Pillsbury's Best Self-Rising Flour, decrease baking powder to ½ teaspoon and salt to ¼ teaspoon.

A hefty main dish that's filling and nutritious. Start it about an hour before dinner.

Southern Corn Beef Pie

 I-pound can corned beef hash
 I-pound can cream-style corn
¼ cup chopped green pepper
 2 tablespoons instant minced onion
 I teaspoon prepared mustard
1½ teaspoons salt
 ½ teaspoon Worcestershire sauce
 ⅛ teaspoon pepper
 I cup Pillsbury's Best All Purpose Flour*
 I cup corn meal
¼ cup sugar
 I tablespoon baking powder
¾ cup milk
¼ cup cooking oil
 I egg
 2 slices uncooked bacon, cut in ½-inch
  pieces

OVEN 425°   6 TO 8 SERVINGS

Combine hash, corn, green pepper, onion, mustard, ½ teaspoon salt, Worcestershire sauce and pepper. Set aside.

Combine flour, corn meal, sugar, baking powder and I teaspoon salt in mixing bowl. Combine milk, oil and egg. Add to dry ingredients all at once, stirring only until moistened. Spread half of mixture in bottom of greased 9-inch square pan. Cover with hash-corn mixture. Top with remaining batter; then with bacon. Bake at 425° for 35 to 40 minutes.

*For use with Pillsbury's Best Self-Rising Flour, decrease baking powder to 1½ teaspoons and salt to ½ teaspoon.

Tiny golden brown drop biscuits ride high on this tomatoey-tuna hot-dish. A good cupboard shelf recipe that can be made in an hour.

Polynesian Tuna Bake

 ⅔ cup chopped green pepper
10½-ounce can condensed tomato soup
 2 tablespoons brown sugar
 I tablespoon instant minced onion
 I teaspoon grated lemon peel
 3 tablespoons lemon juice
 2 teaspoons soy sauce
 2 (6½-ounce) cans tuna, drained and flaked
 I teaspoon sesame seed

Drop Biscuits
 I cup Pillsbury's Best All Purpose Flour*
1½ teaspoons baking powder
¼ teaspoon salt
 ½ cup milk
 2 tablespoons cooking oil

OVEN 375°   5 TO 6 SERVINGS

Combine green pepper, tomato soup, brown sugar, onion, lemon peel, lemon juice, soy sauce and tuna in an 8 or 9-inch skillet. Simmer, covered, for 10 to 15 minutes while preparing Drop Biscuits. Drop Biscuits by teaspoonfuls on hot mixture. Sprinkle with sesame seed. Bake at 375° for 25 to 30 minutes or until golden brown.

Drop Biscuits: Combine flour, baking powder and salt in mixing bowl. Combine milk and oil. Add to flour mixture, stir until dough forms.

Tip: If skillet has plastic handle; cover it with foil.

*For use with Pillsbury's Best Self-Rising Flour, omit baking powder and salt.

Try new "toppings" for your favorite casseroles such as crushed potato chips, grated cheese or dry cereal crumbs.

MENU

Family Supper
Chuckwagon Round-Up
Buttered Peas
Tossed Salad
Pudding with Fruit
Crisp Cookie
Beverage

Shaped like a wagon-wheel in a pie pan and served in "spoked" wedges. Round-up time in one hour.

Chuckwagon Round-Up

¾ cup Pillsbury's Best All Purpose Flour*
1½ teaspoons baking powder
½ teaspoon salt
¼ teaspoon chili powder
⅓ cup milk
2 tablespoons cooking oil
1 egg
½ pound frankfurters
1-pound can barbecue beans
½ cup shredded Cheddar cheese
2 tablespoons dairy sour cream
½ teaspoon onion powder
½ teaspoon leaf oregano

OVEN 375°   4 TO 6 SERVINGS

Combine flour, baking powder, salt and chili powder in mixing bowl. Combine milk, oil and egg. Add to dry ingredients all at once stirring until well mixed. Spread on bottom and sides of greased 9-inch pie pan.

Reserve 2 frankfurters; cut remainder in ½-inch slices. Combine with beans, cheese, sour cream, onion powder and oregano. Spoon filling in center of dough in pie pan. Cut the two reserved frankfurters in half lengthwise and then crosswise. Place over filling, skin side up, in spoke fashion. Bake at 375° for 30 to 35 minutes. Let stand 10 minutes before cutting in wedges and serving.

*For use with Pillsbury's Best Self-Rising Flour, omit baking powder and salt.

Dried beef gets a golden cheese sauce and cheese-and-onion biscuits. You can do it in forty-five minutes.

Creamed Beef Cheezy

¼ cup butter
⅓ cup Pillsbury's Best All Purpose or
    Self-Rising Flour
3 cups milk
½ pound sliced dried beef, shredded
¾ cup shredded Cheddar cheese
1 teaspoon dried parsley flakes

Biscuits

1 cup Pillsbury's Best All Purpose Flour*
2 teaspoons baking powder
1 teaspoon instant minced onion
¼ teaspoon salt
⅓ cup buttermilk
3 tablespoons cooking oil

OVEN 400°   5 TO 6 SERVINGS

Melt butter in medium saucepan. Blend in flour. Add milk gradually. Cook over medium heat, stirring constantly, until thickened. Remove from heat. Add dried beef and ¼ cup cheese. Stir until cheese melts. Pour into a greased 9-inch square or 1½-quart baking dish. Top with Biscuits. Bake at 400° for 20 to 25 minutes. Sprinkle with ½ cup cheese and parsley. Bake 3 minutes longer. Serve hot.

Biscuits: Combine flour, baking powder, onion and salt in a small mixing bowl. Combine buttermilk and oil. Add to dry ingredients all at once, stirring until dough clings together. Knead on lightly floured surface 10 times. Roll out to a ⅜-inch thickness. Cut into rounds with floured 1½-inch biscuit cutter.

Tips: If desired, omit biscuits and serve hot over toast.

To shred dried beef, cut in thin strips with kitchen shears.

*For use with Pillsbury's Best Self-Rising Flour, omit baking powder and salt.

Pink salmon and green peas set sail in a biscuit-pastry that is quite unusual. Start this an hour before dinner.

Salmon-Cheese Pie

2 cups Pillsbury's Best All Purpose Flour*
1 tablespoon baking powder
½ teaspoon salt
¼ cup milk
¼ cup cooking oil
2 eggs
1-pound can salmon, drained and flaked
10½-ounce can condensed cream of celery
    soup
½ teaspoon Worcestershire sauce
¼ teaspoon onion powder
2 cups drained cooked peas
4-ounces sliced American cheese

Vegetable Sauce

½ teaspoon dry mustard
⅓ cup milk

OVEN 375°   6 SERVINGS

Combine flour, baking powder and salt in large mixing bowl. Blend together milk, oil and eggs. Add to dry ingredients all at once, stirring until dough clings together. Knead lightly on floured surface 8 times. Roll out ⅔ of dough on floured surface to an 11-inch circle. Fit into 9-inch pie pan trimming even with edge of pan.

Flake salmon into bowl, removing skin and bones. Add ½ cup soup, Worcestershire sauce and onion powder. Spread in bottom of pastry-lined pan. Spread with drained peas. Top with cheese slices. Roll out remaining dough to a 9-inch circle. Place on top of cheese. Bake at 375° for 25 to 30 minutes. Serve with Vegetable Sauce.

Vegetable Sauce: Combine remainder of soup with dry mustard and milk. Heat.

*For use with Pillsbury's Best Self-Rising Flour, omit baking powder and salt.

Gold Rush Brunch

1¼ cups Pillsbury Hash Brown Potatoes
¼ cup chopped onion
1 tablespoon dried parsley flakes
2 tablespoons butter
¼ cup flour
½ teaspoon salt
⅛ teaspoon pepper
¾ cup milk
½ cup dairy sour cream
½ to ¾ pound (8 slices) Canadian-style bacon
4 eggs

OVEN 350°   4 SERVINGS

Prepare potatoes according to package directions; drain well. Stir in onion and parsley. Place in greased 9-inch square baking dish. Melt butter in saucepan; blend in flour, salt and pepper. Add milk. Cook over low heat, stirring constantly, until thickened. Remove from heat; blend in sour cream. Pour over potatoes, lifting potatoes lightly to permit sauce to mix well. Arrange bacon in an overlapping row down center of dish. Bake at 350° for 45 minutes. Remove from oven. Make 2 indentations on each side of bacon; slip 1 egg carefully into each indentation. Season with salt and pepper as desired. Bake 15 to 20 minutes longer or until eggs are set.

Tip: Potato and sauce mixture may be made ahead of time, covered and refrigerated. Add bacon just before placing in oven and bake an additional 5 minutes.

Sunday Supper Foldovers

15-ounce can corned beef hash
½ cup drained cooked whole kernel corn
¼ cup chopped green pepper
1 tablespoon instant minced onion
1 tablespoon prepared mustard
¼ teaspoon pepper
1 can Pillsbury Refrigerated Hungry Jack Flaky or Flaky Buttermilk Biscuits

Sauce
10½-ounce can condensed cream of celery soup
⅔ cup milk
1 teaspoon dill seed
⅛ teaspoon pepper

OVEN 375°   5 SERVINGS

Combine hash, corn, green pepper, onion, mustard and pepper.

Open can; separate dough into 10 biscuits. On greased cookie sheet press each biscuit into a 5-inch circle. Place ¼ cup corned beef filling in center of each biscuit, forming filling in rounded "V" shape. Bring opposite sides up over filling overlapping in center. Fasten with toothpick. Bake at 375° for 20 to 25 minutes until golden brown. Serve hot with Sauce.

Sauce: Combine soup, milk, dill seed and pepper in saucepan. Simmer 5 minutes.

The dough comes up around the frankfurters in this colorful and tasty dish. Supper will be served in about forty-five minutes.

Fancy Franks

6 frankfurters
1 tablespoon prepared mustard
¾ cup creamed cottage cheese
¾ cup Pillsbury's Best All Purpose Flour*
2 teaspoons sugar
1½ teaspoons baking powder
½ teaspoon salt
¼ cup milk
2 tablespoons cooking oil or melted bacon fat
1 egg
1 tablespoon catsup
½ cup shredded cheese or 4 slices bacon, cooked and crumbled

OVEN 400°   4 TO 6 SERVINGS

Split frankfurters lengthwise, but do not cut through. Spread cut surface with mustard; top with a rounded tablespoonful of cottage cheese; set aside.

Combine flour, sugar, baking powder and salt in small mixer bowl. Add milk, oil and egg. Blend; then beat at medium speed 2 minutes (or beat 300 strokes with a spoon). Spread on bottom of greased 9x5-inch pan. Arrange frankfurters crosswise in pan, pressing to fit. Drizzle catsup over cottage cheese. Sprinkle with cheese or bacon. Bake at 400° for 30 to 35 minutes until golden brown. Cool 10 minutes; remove to serving platter.

*For use with Pillsbury's Best Self-Rising Flour, omit baking powder and salt.

Savory corn meal muffin mixture is spooned over a frankfurter and bean casserole. A hit with the kids and easy on the budget. One hour.

Teen Bean Bake

  ½ pound frankfurters, cut in ½-inch slices
  2 (1-pound) cans baked beans
  ½ cup catsup
  ½ cup water
  1 tablespoon prepared mustard

<u>Corn Bread Topping</u>
  1 egg, slightly beaten
  ⅔ cup milk
  ¼ cup cooking oil
  ⅓ cup finely chopped onion
  1 cup Pillsbury's Best All Purpose Flour*
  ⅔ cup corn meal
  1 tablespoon sugar
  1½ teaspoons baking powder
  1 teaspoon salt

OVEN 400°   8 TO 10 SERVINGS

Combine frankfurters, baked beans, catsup, water and mustard in a 12x8-inch baking dish. Spoon Corn Bread Topping over beans and bake at 400° for 35 to 40 minutes.

<u>Corn Bread Topping</u>: Combine slightly beaten egg, milk, oil and onion in mixing bowl. Add flour, corn meal, sugar, baking powder and salt. Stir to combine all ingredients.

Tips: 1 can Pillsbury Refrigerated Hungry Jack Flaky or Flaky Buttermilk Biscuits may be used for Corn Bread Topping. Open can; separate dough into 10 biscuits. Dip <u>tops</u> <u>only</u> in milk, then in corn meal and place over bean mixture. Bake at 400° for 30 to 35 minutes.

For a milder flavor, use 1 cup tomato sauce instead of catsup and water.

If desired, substitute one 12-ounce can luncheon meat for frankfurters.

*For use with Pillsbury's Best Self-Rising Flour, omit baking powder and salt.

Ready-prepared foods go together to make you a last-minute genius. Open the first can about an hour before serving time.

Busy Lady Beef Bake

  10-ounce package frozen peas and onions
    in butter sauce
  2 tablespoons flour
  1½-pound can beef stew

<u>Biscuits</u>
  1 cup Pillsbury's Best All Purpose Flour*
  1½ teaspoons baking powder
  ½ teaspoon seasoned salt
  ½ teaspoon sweet basil
  ½ cup milk
  2 tablespoons cooking oil

OVEN 425°   5 TO 6 SERVINGS

Place peas and onions, flour and stew in 2-quart casserole. Cover. Bake at 425° for 25 minutes. Stir. Drop Biscuits by tablespoonfuls around edge of casserole. Bake, uncovered, at 425° for 25 to 30 minutes.

<u>Biscuits</u>: In mixing bowl, combine flour, baking powder, seasoned salt and basil. Combine milk and oil; add to dry ingredients and stir until all dry particles are moistened.

*For use with Pillsbury's Best Self-Rising Flour, omit baking powder and seasoned salt.

Snappy flavor, snappy to make, with color and tang in both the casserole and the topping. Takes about sixty minutes from start to serving.

Calico Casserole

    2 (15¼-ounce) cans meatballs in gravy
    1-pound can mixed vegetables, drained
    10-ounce package frozen small onions
      in cream sauce
    1 teaspoon chili powder
    ¼ teaspoon pepper

Chili Biscuits

    1 cup Pillsbury's Best All Purpose Flour*
    2 teaspoons baking powder
    1 teaspoon chili powder
    ½ teaspoon salt
    ¼ cup milk
    2 tablespoons cooking oil
    1 egg
    1 cup shredded Cheddar cheese
    ½ cup sliced stuffed green olives
    ½ cup slivered blanched almonds, if desired
    ½ teaspoon Worcestershire sauce

OVEN 425°   6 TO 8 SERVINGS

Combine meatballs in gravy, mixed vegetables, onions, chili powder and pepper in 12x8-inch baking dish. Bake uncovered at 425° for 20 minutes. Prepare Chili Biscuits. Remove casserole from oven; stir. Place biscuits, cut-side up along 12-inch sides of baking dish. Bake 25 to 30 minutes longer.

Chili Biscuits: Combine flour, baking powder, chili powder and salt in mixing bowl. Combine milk, oil and egg; add to dry ingredients all at once, stirring until dough clings together. Knead lightly on floured surface 8 times. Roll out to a 12x9-inch rectangle. Combine cheese, olives, almonds and Worcestershire sauce. Spread over dough. Starting with 12-inch side, roll up jelly roll fashion; seal edge. Cut into 1-inch slices.

Tip: For quick biscuits, use 1 can Pillsbury Refrigerated Quick Crescent Dinner Rolls. Add 1 teaspoon chili powder to cheese-olive filling. Open can; unroll dough to form 4 rectangles. Spread with filling. Roll-up. Cut each in 3 slices and place on hot casserole. Bake at 400° for 25 to 30 minutes.

*For use with Pillsbury's Best Self-Rising Flour, omit baking powder and salt.

Biscuit toppings should be placed on a piping hot main dish to help speed their baking and prevent sogginess.

Don't hesitate to prepare two casseroles, freezing one for future use.

The popular frankfurter-in-crescent roll idea, done with dash and in only thirty minutes.

Hot Ziggities

   8 frankfurters
   4 teaspoons prepared mustard
   1 can Pillsbury Refrigerated Quick Crescent
     Dinner Rolls
   2 tablespoons barbecue sauce or catsup

OVEN 375°   4 TO 6 SERVINGS

Cut frankfurters in half lengthwise. Spread cut edges with mustard. Place back together. Unroll dough; separate into 8 triangles. Place frankfurters on wide end of triangle and roll up. Place on ungreased cookie sheet. Brush with barbecue sauce or catsup. Bake at 375° for 15 to 20 minutes until golden brown. Serve hot.

Basic ingredients should always be measured accurately. Seasonings may be varied in amount to suit family tastes.

This is something like a "Parmesan cream puff" that bakes right onto the chops. Give yourself an hour and a quarter.

Parmesan Puff Chops

    4 pork chops
    ½ teaspoon salt

<u>Cheese Topping</u>
    2 tablespoons shortening
    ½ cup Pillsbury's Best All Purpose Flour*
    ½ teaspoon baking powder
    ⅔ cup milk
    2 eggs
    ⅓ cup grated Parmesan cheese
    2 tablespoons instant minced onion
    ½ teaspoon salt
    ¼ teaspoon pepper
    Paprika, if desired

OVEN 350°   4 SERVINGS

Arrange pork chops in a 9-inch square baking dish or skillet. Place in 350° oven while preparing Cheese Topping. Sprinkle with salt. Turn chops over, spread with Cheese Topping to cover completely. Sprinkle lightly with paprika, if desired. Bake at 350° for about I hour or until golden brown.

<u>Cheese Topping</u>: Melt shortening in a medium saucepan. Blend in flour and baking powder. Gradually add milk. Cook over medium heat, stirring constantly until very thick. Remove from heat and blend in unbeaten eggs, one at a time. Cook over low heat, beating hard until very thick. Remove from heat. Add Parmesan cheese, onion, salt and pepper. Blend thoroughly.

*For use with Pillsbury's Best Self-Rising Flour, omit baking powder and salt.

A "different" pizza, topped with frankfurters and bean with bacon soup. Ready, crust and all, in about an hour.

Pauper's Pizza

    ½ cup buttermilk
    I tablespoon sugar
    I tablespoon butter
    I package active dry yeast
    I to 1¼ cups Pillsbury's Best All Purpose Flour*
    ½ teaspoon salt
    ⅛ teaspoon soda
    I cup shredded Cheddar cheese

<u>Topping</u>
    10½-ounce can condensed bean with bacon soup
    ¼ cup catsup
    2 tablespoons prepared mustard
    I tablespoon instant minced onion
    I pound frankfurters, cut in ½-inch slices

OVEN 400°   6 SERVINGS

Combine buttermilk, sugar and butter in medium saucepan. Heat, stirring constantly, to lukewarm. Remove from heat. Add yeast; stir to dissolve. Stir in flour, salt and soda until blended and forms a stiff dough. Knead on floured surface until smooth, about I minute. Place dough on greased 12-inch pizza pan or cookie sheet. Cover; let rest 10 minutes while combining ingredients for Topping. Pat out dough to a 12-inch circle. Spread Topping to edge of dough; sprinkle with cheese. Bake on bottom rack in oven at 400° for 20 to 25 minutes. Cool 10 minutes before cutting in wedges and serving.

<u>Topping</u>: Combine all ingredients; mix well.

*For use with Pillsbury's Best Self-Rising Flour, omit salt.

Saturday Night Pie

2 (1-pound) jars potato salad
1 cup drained sauerkraut
½ pound cocktail frankfurters
½ teaspoon salt
½ teaspoon caraway seed
Paprika

OVEN 400°   6 SERVINGS

Combine potato salad, sauerkraut, frankfurters (reserve about 8 frankfurters for top), salt and caraway seed in large mixing bowl. Mix well. Place mixture in 9-inch pie pan or 1½-quart baking dish. Arrange reserved frankfurters on top and sprinkle with paprika. Bake at 400° for 25 to 30 minutes.

73

A meal-in-one, topped with packaged pie crust. Put it in the oven two and a half hours before dinner and you've got it made.

One Step Beef Pie

    I pound stewing beef, cut in I-inch cubes
    2 tablespoons flour
    I package Pillsbury Brown Gravy Mix
    2 medium onions, sliced
    2 cups sliced raw potatoes
    I cup sliced raw carrots
    I½ cups water
    I teaspoon salt
    ⅛ teaspoon pepper
    ½ teaspoon Worcestershire sauce
    I package Pillsbury Flaky Pie Crust Sticks

OVEN 400°   4 TO 6 SERVINGS

Place meat on bottom of 9-inch square baking dish. Sprinkle with flour and dry gravy mix, toss to coat. Top with onions, potatoes and carrots. Combine water, salt, pepper and Worcestershire sauce. Pour over meat and vegetables. Prepare one pie crust stick as directed on package. Roll out to 10-inch square. Cut slits for escape of steam. Place over filling and flute edges. Bake at 400° for 20 minutes. Reduce temperature and bake at 350° for I½ to 2 hours or until meat is tender.

Tip: If desired, use Single Crust Pastry recipe, see page 5

Combine flour, baking powder and salt in mixing bowl. Add mayonnaise and milk; stir until mixture forms a ball. Sprinkle I table-spoon sesame seed in bottom of a 9-inch pie pan. Press dough in bottom and sides of pie pan. Spread with barbecue sauce. Arrange frankfurters over sauce pressing into sauce. Sprinkle with cheese and remaining I table-spoon sesame seed. Bake at 425° for 20 to 25 minutes. Cool 10 minutes before cutting in wedges and serving.

*For use with Pillsbury's Best Self-Rising Flour, omit baking powder and salt.

Tamales take on a new look with a cheesy, corn meal topping "polka-dotted" with ripe olives. Dinner Olé in less than an hour.

Caballero Casserole

    15-ounce can beef tamales in sauce
    12-ounce can whole kernel corn with sweet peppers, drained
    10½-ounce can pizza sauce

<u>*Cheese Olive Topping*</u>
    ⅓ cup corn meal
    ¼ cup flour
    1⅜-ounce packet cheese sauce mix
    I teaspoon sugar
    ¾ teaspoon baking powder
    I egg
    ½ cup milk
    2 tablespoons cooking oil
    2 tablespoons chopped ripe olives

OVEN 400°   6 SERVINGS

Cut each tamale into 6 pieces. Place tamales and sauce in bottom of 9-inch square baking dish. Top with corn; then pizza sauce. Pour Cheese Olive Topping over casserole. Bake at 400° for 30 to 35 minutes.

<u>Cheese Olive Topping</u>: Combine dry ingredients in mixing bowl. Add remaining ingredients; stir until well mixed.

They'll never guess all the ingredients of this spicy, cheese topped dish. Ready-to-serve in wedges in less than an hour.

The Works Casserole

    I cup Pillsbury's Best All Purpose Flour*
    ½ teaspoon baking powder
    ½ teaspoon salt
    ⅓ cup mayonnaise
    ¼ cup milk
    2 tablespoons sesame seed
    15¼-ounce can barbecue sauce with beef
    ½ pound frankfurters, cut in ½-inch pieces
    I cup (4-ounces) shredded Mozzarella cheese

Even pork is better the second time around! Topped with corn bread for a hearty gold finish in an hour and a half.

Pork and Corn Bread Bake

    I pound cubed pork
    2 (8-ounce) cans tomato sauce
    I-pound can whole kernel corn, drained
    ½ teaspoon salt

<u>Topping</u>
    ½ cup Pillsbury's Best All Purpose Flour*
    ½ cup corn meal
    I tablespoon sugar
    2 teaspoons baking powder
    ½ teaspoon salt
    I tablespoon sweet pepper flakes
    ½ cup milk
    I egg
    2 tablespoons cooking oil

OVEN 400°   6 TO 8 SERVINGS

Place pork in 2-quart casserole. Bake uncovered at 400° for 45 minutes. Stir in tomato sauce, corn and salt. Pour Topping over pork mixture. Bake at 400° for 35 to 40 minutes.

Topping: Combine flour, corn meal, sugar, baking powder, salt and pepper flakes in mixing bowl. Combine milk, egg and oil. Add to dry ingredients all at once; stirring just until blended.

Tip: If desired, use 2 cups cubed leftover cooked pork.

*For use with Pillsbury's Best Self-Rising Flour, decrease baking powder to I teaspoon and salt to ¼ teaspoon.

Delightful new version of plain old tomato sauce and frankfurters. Table-ready in an hour and a quarter.

Pennsylvania Knockbockle

    ½ pound frankfurters, cut in ¼-inch
       diagonal slices
    2 tablespoons sweet pepper flakes
    2 tablespoons dry onion flakes
    8-ounce can spaghetti sauce with
       mushrooms
    4-ounce can mushroom stems and pieces,
       drained
    ¼ cup water

<u>Potato Topping</u>
    4-serving recipe Pillsbury Hungry Jack
       Mashed Potatoes
    I egg, slightly beaten
    ¼ cup grated Parmesan cheese

OVEN 400°   4 SERVINGS

Combine frankfurters, sweet pepper flakes, onion flakes, spaghetti sauce, mushrooms and water in a I-quart casserole. Cover and bake at 400° for 30 minutes. Drop Potato Topping by tablespoonfuls around edge of casserole. Sprinkle with additional Parmesan cheese and potato flakes. Bake at 400° for 20 to 25 minutes until golden brown.

Potato Topping: Prepare 4-serving recipe mashed potatoes as directed on package using I cup water. Blend in egg and Parmesan cheese.

Best Chicken and Turkey Recipes

• The flavors of chicken and turkey are subtle and many, and each of the recipes on the following pages has put a new slant on this popular poultry.

If your bird is already cooked, you have merely to cut it up. However, if you're starting from scratch, you will find a basic recipe for stewing a chicken on page four. The best method of defrosting a frozen chicken is *slowly,* in the refrigerator. It will lose much less of its juice and flavor.

Thanks to advances in modern poultry raising, chicken and turkey are available at popular prices throughout the year . . . fresh or frozen, whole or in parts. Enjoy them often.

Chunks of chicken in wine sauce with sour cream potatoes. Ready in an hour. For a crowd see page 96.

Chicken Almond Party Bake

10½-ounce can condensed cream of chicken
    soup
  4-ounce can mushroom stems and pieces,
    drained
  3 cups cubed cooked chicken
  ½ cup white cooking wine or chicken broth
  ½ cup blanched slivered almonds
  ¼ cup chopped pimiento
  1 teaspoon instant minced onion
  ½ teaspoon salt

Potato Topping
  1 cup water
  2 tablespoons butter
  ½ teaspoon salt
  ¼ cup milk
  1½ cups Pillsbury Hungry Jack Mashed
    Potato Flakes
  ½ cup dairy sour cream
  1 egg

OVEN 375°   4 TO 6 SERVINGS

Combine soup, mushrooms, chicken, wine, ¼ cup almonds, pimiento, onion and salt in 8-inch square baking dish. Drop Potato Topping by tablespoonfuls on filling. Sprinkle with remaining ¼ cup almonds. Bake at 375° for 40 to 45 minutes until golden brown.

Potato Topping: Heat water, butter and salt to boiling in saucepan. Remove from heat. Add milk, stir in potato flakes with fork just until moistened. Let stand until liquid is absorbed (about ½ minute). Blend in sour cream. Add egg and blend well.

Tips: Make up to 12 hours ahead. Cover and refrigerate. Bake at 375° for 45 to 50 minutes.

If canned chicken is used, reduce first baking to 15 to 20 minutes or until mixture is bubbly.

This may be your leftover turkey's finest hour, (that's all the time it takes), with almonds, pimiento and a terrific topping.

Hot Turkey Hustle Up

10½-ounce can condensed cream of
    mushroom soup
3 cups cubed cooked turkey
1 cup finely chopped celery
½ cup blanched slivered almonds
½ cup mayonnaise
1 tablespoon lemon juice
3 hard-cooked eggs, sliced
3 tablespoons chopped pimiento
2 teaspoons dried onion flakes
½ teaspoon monosodium glutamate
½ teaspoon salt

Topping
½ cup Pillsbury's Best All Purpose Flour*
½ cup sesame seed
¼ cup shredded American cheese
¼ teaspoon salt
¼ cup butter, melted

OVEN 375°   6 TO 8 SERVINGS

Combine ingredients in 9-inch square baking dish. Sprinkle with Topping. Bake at 375° for 25 to 30 minutes.

Topping: Combine all ingredients; mix thoroughly.

*For use with Pillsbury's Best Self-Rising Flour, omit salt.

Oven-fried chicken, dumplings and sauce all in one pan. Ready in an hour and forty-five minutes.

Chicken Easy Casserole

2½ to 3 pound frying chicken, cut into pieces
¼ cup flour
1½ teaspoons salt
1 teaspoon paprika
½ teaspoon ginger
10½-ounce can condensed cream of
    mushroom soup
1 cup water

Dumpling Topping
¾ cup Pillsbury's Best All Purpose Flour*
¼ cup corn meal
1 tablespoon sugar
2 teaspoons baking powder
½ teaspoon salt
¼ teaspoon ginger
¼ cup milk
2 eggs

OVEN 350°   6 SERVINGS

Coat chicken with mixture of flour, salt, paprika and ginger. Place skin side up in 13x9-inch baking pan. Combine soup and water until well blended. Pour over chicken in baking pan. Bake uncovered at 350° for 1 hour. Remove from oven, increase oven temperature to 400°. Drop Dumpling Topping by tablespoonfuls between pieces of chicken. Bake uncovered at 400° for 20 to 25 minutes.

Dumpling Topping: Combine flour, corn meal, sugar, baking powder, salt and ginger in mixing bowl. Combine milk and eggs. Add to dry ingredients; mix only until smooth.

*For use with Pillsbury's Best Self-Rising Flour, omit baking powder and salt.

White grapes, raisins and spices make this something special. A deliciously different casserole ready in about an hour.

Sunshine Chicken Casserole

10½-ounce can condensed cream of celery
    soup
  8-ounce can white grapes, drained
  2 cups diced cooked chicken
  ½ cup golden raisins
  ½ cup dairy sour cream
  1 tablespoon brown sugar
  2 tablespoons chopped pimiento
  ½ teaspoon salt
  ⅛ teaspoon cinnamon
 ¹/₁₆ teaspoon ground cloves
  2 hard-cooked eggs, sliced

Drop Biscuits
  ¾ cup Pillsbury's Best All Purpose Flour*
  1 teaspoon baking powder
  ½ teaspoon salt
  ¼ teaspoon soda
  ¼ teaspoon celery seed
  ½ cup dairy sour cream
  1 egg
  3 drops yellow food coloring, if desired

OVEN 400°   6 SERVINGS

Combine soup, grapes, chicken, raisins, sour cream, brown sugar, pimiento, salt, cinnamon, cloves and eggs in 2-quart casserole. Cover. Bake at 400° for 20 minutes. Remove from oven; stir to blend. Drop Biscuits by tablespoonfuls around edge of casserole. Bake at 400° for 20 to 25 minutes.

Drop Biscuits: Combine flour, baking powder, salt, soda and celery seed in mixing bowl. Combine sour cream, egg and yellow food coloring. Add to dry ingredients, all at once, stirring only until moistened.

*For use with Pillsbury's Best Self-Rising Flour, omit baking powder and salt.

Zing up left-over turkey with oysters (of all things) and cranberry sauce. Only forty-five minutes to prepare, and it can be made ahead.

Turkey Gobbler

10½-ounce can condensed cream of celery
    soup
  8-ounce can oysters, drained and reserve
    liquid
  2 cups diced cooked turkey
  1 tablespoon chopped pimiento
  ½ cup cubed jellied cranberry sauce

Crumb Topping
  2 tablespoons butter, melted
  ½ cup coarse corn flake crumbs

OVEN 400°   5 SERVINGS

Combine soup and oyster liquid in 1½-quart casserole. Add turkey, pimiento and oysters. Mix well. Sprinkle with Crumb Topping; top with cubes of jellied cranberry sauce. Bake at 400° for 20 to 25 minutes.

Crumb Topping: Combine melted butter and corn flake crumbs.

Tip: This can be made ahead, covered and refrigerated. Bake, uncovered, at 400° for 25 to 30 minutes.

Maryland Chicken Supper

10½-ounce can condensed cream of chicken
    soup
  4-ounce can mushroom stems and pieces,
    drained
  3 cups cubed cooked chicken
  ¾ cup dairy sour cream
  ½ cup chopped onion
  ½ cup chopped celery
    I teaspoon salt
    I teaspoon Worcestershire sauce
  ⅛ teaspoon pepper

Drop Biscuits
  ½ cup Pillsbury's Best All Purpose Flour*
    I teaspoon baking powder
  ¼ teaspoon salt
  ½ cup shredded cheese
    I tablespoon chopped pimiento
    I teaspoon dried parsley flakes
  2 tablespoons milk
    I egg

OVEN 400°   4 TO 5 SERVINGS

Combine soup, mushrooms, chicken, sour cream, onion, celery, salt, Worcestershire sauce and pepper in I½-quart casserole. Cover. Bake at 400° for 30 minutes. Remove from oven. Stir to mix well. Drop Biscuits by tablespoonfuls around edge of casserole. Bake at 400° for an additional 20 to 25 minutes until golden brown.

Drop Biscuits: Combine flour, baking powder, salt, cheese, pimiento and parsley in mixing bowl. Combine milk and egg. Add to dry ingredients, mixing only until blended.

Tip: *If you prefer more biscuit topping, use a 2-quart casserole, double the biscuit recipe and bake at 400° for 30 to 35 minutes.*

*For use with Pillsbury's Best Self-Rising Flour, omit baking powder and salt.

Chicken Mexicano

10½-ounce can condensed cream of
    mushroom soup
  ½ cup milk
    I tablespoon instant minced onion
    I tablespoon dried parsley flakes
  ½ to I teaspoon chili powder
  ½ teaspoon garlic salt
  ¼ teaspoon hot pepper sauce
  3 cups cubed cooked chicken
  4-ounce can mushroom stems and pieces,
    drained
  ½ cup chopped green or ripe olives
  ¼ cup chopped pimiento
  ¼ cup slivered almonds

Potato Puff Topping
  4-serving recipe Pillsbury Hungry Jack
    Mashed Potatoes
    I egg, slightly beaten

OVEN 400°   6 SERVINGS

Combine soup, milk, onion, parsley, chili powder, garlic salt, hot pepper sauce, chicken, mushrooms, olives and pimiento. Spread over bottom of 8-inch square baking dish. Prepare Potato Puff Topping. Drop by tablespoonfuls over chicken mixture. Sprinkle with almonds. Bake at 400° for 25 to 30 minutes until potatoes are golden brown.

Potato Puff Topping: Prepare 4-serving recipe mashed potatoes as directed on package, using I cup water. Blend in egg.

A crust made with dressing will make this a conversation topic at your luncheon. Begin it an hour and a half before serving time.

Chicken 'N Dressing Pie

4 cups dry bread cubes
½ teaspoon salt
½ teaspoon poultry seasoning
¼ cup butter, melted
I egg

Filling

2 eggs
2 cups cubed cooked chicken
8-ounce can cream style corn
4-ounce can mushroom stems and pieces, drained
½ cup finely chopped celery
¼ cup chopped pimiento
I teaspoon instant minced onion
½ teaspoon salt
¼ teaspoon poultry seasoning
⅛ teaspoon pepper

OVEN 350°   5 TO 6 SERVINGS

Combine bread cubes, salt, poultry seasoning and melted butter. Toss to mix. Reserve I cup. Add egg to remainder; mix well. Lightly press to cover bottom and sides of greased 9-inch pie pan. Pour in Filling. Sprinkle reserved bread cubes over top, pressing into Filling lightly. Bake at 350° for 40 to 45 minutes. Cool I0 minutes. Spoon or cut in wedges to serve.

Filling: Beat eggs slightly. Blend in remaining ingredients.

Tip: If desired, serve with Pillsbury Chicken Gravy Mix prepared as directed on package.

Chicken Curry Croquettes

10½-ounce can condensed cream of chicken
    soup
  1 cup Pillsbury Hungry Jack Mashed Potato
    Flakes
  2 cups finely diced or ground cooked
    chicken
  ¼ cup finely chopped celery
  1 tablespoon dried parsley flakes
  1 tablespoon lemon juice
  ½ teaspoon instant minced onion
  ¼ to ½ teaspoon curry powder
  ⅛ teaspoon hot pepper sauce
  2 eggs

Coating

  2 eggs, slightly beaten
  ¼ cup milk
  ¼ teaspoon curry powder
  1¼ cups dry bread crumbs

Mushroom Sauce

10½-ounce can condensed cream of
    mushroom soup
  ½ cup milk
  ½ teaspoon instant minced onion
  ⅛ to ¼ teaspoon curry powder

DEEP FAT 325°   5 TO 6 SERVINGS

Combine soup, potato flakes, chicken, celery, parsley flakes, lemon juice, onion, curry powder and hot pepper sauce in a bowl. Stir in eggs. Place mixture in shallow pan, cover and place in freezer for 2 to 3 hours until partially frozen. Prepare Coating mixture and Mushroom Sauce. Shape croquettes using 1 heaping tablespoonful for each croquette. Roll in dry bread crumbs, then dip in egg mixture and roll in crumbs again. Fry in deep hot fat (325°) for 4 to 5 minutes or until golden brown. Drain on absorbent paper. Serve immediately with Mushroom Sauce.

Coating: Combine egg, milk and curry powder in a bowl. Place dry bread crumbs in a shallow dish or pan.

Mushroom Sauce: Combine soup, milk, onion and curry powder in a saucepan. Heat thoroughly.

Tip: Shape croquettes and roll in egg and crumb mixture ahead of time. Store in refrigerator until ready to fry.

Croquettes with the exotic pinch of curry, and do-ahead convenience. Allow two to three hours for chilling.

Water chestnuts add a crunchy goodness to this "hot salad". Ready for Freddie in forty-five minutes.

Chicken Salad Bake

  2 cups cubed cooked chicken
  1 cup chopped celery
  ½ cup chopped onion
  5-ounce can water chestnuts, drained and
    sliced
  ½ cup shredded Cheddar cheese
  ½ cup mayonnaise
  1 tablespoon lemon juice
  ½ teaspoon salt
  ⅛ teaspoon pepper
  1 cup canned shoestring potatoes

OVEN 400°   4 TO 5 SERVINGS

Combine chicken, celery, onion, water chestnuts, Cheddar cheese, mayonnaise, lemon juice, salt and pepper in 1½-quart casserole. Sprinkle with shoestring potatoes. Bake at 400° for 20 to 25 minutes.

Tip: Potato chips or chow mein noodles may be substituted for the shoestring potatoes.

Full of savory tidbits that make it out of the ordinary. Nestled inside of a flavorful parsley'd crust. Prepare it in an hour.

City Slicker Chickerole

2 cups cubed cooked chicken
2 cups frozen French fried potatoes
1-pound can cut green beans, drained
10½-ounce can condensed cream of chicken
    soup
1 package Pillsbury Chicken Gravy Mix
⅓ cup sliced stuffed olives
1 teaspoon salt
⅔ cup dairy sour cream
⅓ cup slivered almonds
⅔ cup shredded sharp cheese

Crust
½ cup shortening
½ cup catsup
2 cups Pillsbury's Best All Purpose Flour*
2 teaspoons dried parsley flakes
1 teaspoon baking powder
½ teaspoon salt

OVEN 375°   6 SERVINGS

Combine chicken, potatoes, green beans, soup, gravy mix, olives and salt in large saucepan. Cover and heat over medium heat while preparing Crust. Press dough evenly over bottom and sides of 12x8-inch baking dish or 2-quart casserole. Blend sour cream into chicken mixture; pour into pastry lined casserole. Bake at 375° for 20 to 25 minutes. Sprinkle almonds and cheese over the top. Return to oven for 10 minutes until cheese is melted.

Crust: Melt shortening in saucepan. Add catsup, flour, parsley flakes, baking powder and salt. Mix until mixture forms dough and pulls from sides of pan.

*For use with Pillsbury's Best Self-Rising Flour, omit baking powder and salt.

Here's Sunday dinner with the taste of home. The dressing bakes right with it. Begin an hour and three quarters before dinner.

Country Style Chicken Bake

¼ cup butter
3 pound frying chicken, cut into pieces
¼ cup flour
1½ teaspoons salt
¼ teaspoon pepper
1 cup chopped onion
1 cup chopped celery
3 chicken bouillon cubes
1½ cups boiling water

Topping
¾ cup Pillsbury's Best All Purpose Flour*
¼ cup corn meal
2 teaspoons baking powder
½ teaspoon salt
½ to 1 teaspoon poultry seasoning
½ cup milk
2 eggs

OVEN 400°   6 SERVINGS

Melt butter in 13x9-inch pan. Coat chicken with mixture of flour, salt and pepper. Dip skin side of chicken in butter; place skin side up in pan. Sprinkle chopped onion and celery between chicken pieces lifting pieces to allow it to go underneath. Bake at 400° for 1 hour. Remove from oven. Pour Topping between pieces of chicken. Dissolve bouillon cubes in boiling water. Pour over chicken and Topping. Bake at 400° for 20 to 25 minutes until golden.

Topping: Combine flour, corn meal, baking powder, salt and poultry seasoning in mixing bowl. Combine milk and eggs. Add to dry ingredients all at once, stirring only until smooth.

*For use with Pillsbury's Best Self-Rising Flour, omit baking powder and salt.

For the beautiful luncheon: this hot egg-noodle chicken loaf, garnished to a fare-thee-well. Start an hour and a half ahead or make early in the day.

Party Chicken Loaf

4-ounces egg noodles

½ cup chopped celery

¼ cup chopped green pepper

¼ cup butter or chicken fat

¼ cup Pillsbury's Best All Purpose or
Self-Rising Flour

13¾-ounce can chicken broth or 1⅔ cups milk

2 tablespoons chopped pimiento

1½ teaspoons salt

1 teaspoon Worcestershire sauce

⅛ teaspoon pepper

3 cups cubed cooked chicken

3 eggs, slightly beaten

OVEN 350° 6 TO 8 SERVINGS

Cook noodles as directed on package. Drain. In a large skillet sauté celery and green pepper in butter until tender, about 5 minutes. Blend in flour. Gradually stir in chicken broth, pimiento, salt, Worcestershire sauce and pepper.

Cook over medium heat, stirring constantly until mixture boils. Boil 1 minute. Add noodles, chicken and eggs. Blend well. Pour into greased 9x5-inch baking pan. Set in pan containing at least 1-inch hot water. Bake at 350° for 70 to 75 minutes or until knife inserted in center comes out clean. Cool 10 minutes. Loosen edge with spatula. Invert on serving platter. Garnish with parsley and pimiento, if desired.

Tip: Prepare ahead, cover and refrigerate. Bake at 350° for 85 to 90 minutes.

MENU

Holiday or Spring Buffet
Party Chicken Loaf
Buttered Whole Baby Carrots
Tossed Salad
Assorted Hot Breads
Strawberry Shortcake
Beverage

Chicken A La Cheese Pie

¾ cup milk
I package Pillsbury Chicken Gravy Mix
¼ cup chopped green pepper
3 cups cubed cooked chicken
I teaspoon chopped chives
¼ teaspoon salt
⅛ teaspoon pepper
I cup shredded Cheddar or Swiss cheese

Crust
½ cup Pillsbury's Best All Purpose Flour*
½ cup Pillsbury Hungry Jack Mashed Potato Flakes
I teaspoon baking powder
½ teaspoon salt
½ cup water
⅓ cup shortening
I egg

OVEN 400°   6 SERVINGS

Combine milk and gravy mix in saucepan. Add green pepper and cook over medium heat, stirring constantly until thickened. Stir in chicken, chives, salt and pepper. Spread Crust on bottom and sides of greased 9-inch pie pan. Spoon chicken filling in center. Sprinkle with cheese. Bake at 400° for 40 to 45 minutes. Let cool 10 minutes before cutting in wedges and serving.

Crust: Combine flour, potato flakes, baking powder and salt in small mixer bowl. Add water, shortening and egg. Blend at low speed. Beat at medium speed for 2 minutes.

*For use with Pillsbury's Best Self-Rising Flour, omit baking powder and salt.

Polynesian Buffet Chicken

½ cup butter
2½ to 3 pound frying chicken, cut into pieces
½ cup Pillsbury's Best All Purpose or Self-Rising Flour
2 teaspoons salt
I teaspoon paprika
I teaspoon cinnamon
½ teaspoon ginger
½ teaspoon nutmeg
I egg
8½-ounce can sliced pineapple, drained, reserve liquid
1⅓ cups flaked coconut

OVEN 350°   4 TO 5 SERVINGS

Melt butter in 13x9-inch baking pan. Wash and dry chicken. Combine flour, salt, paprika, cinnamon, ginger and nutmeg in mixing bowl. Add egg and liquid from pineapple slices; beat until well blended. Dip chicken pieces in batter; shake off excess batter; roll skin side in coconut. Dip skin side of chicken in butter; place skin side up in pan. Bake at 350° for 40 minutes. Top with pineapple which has been cut in quarters. Bake 20 to 30 minutes longer until chicken is tender.

Tip: Prepare chicken ahead, place in pan, cover and refrigerate. Bake at 350° for I hour and 10 minutes before serving.

A crunchy corn meal crust encloses the savory chicken in this family size turnover. You can make it in little over an hour.

Giant Chicken Turnover

½ cup chopped onion
½ cup chopped celery
3 tablespoons butter or chicken fat
2 tablespoons flour
½ teaspoon poultry seasoning
½ cup milk
3 cups cubed cooked chicken
1 package Pillsbury Butterflake Recipe
    Pie Crust Mix
⅓ cup corn meal

<u>Sauce</u>

4-ounce can mushroom stems and pieces,
    drained
2 tablespoons butter
¾ cup water
¼ cup milk
1 package Pillsbury Chicken Gravy Mix
2 tablespoons chopped pimiento

OVEN 425°   6 SERVINGS

Sauté onion and celery in butter. Stir in flour and poultry seasoning; slowly blend in milk. Cook, stirring constantly until thickened. Blend in chicken. Set aside. Prepare pie crust mix as directed on package using 5 tablespoons water and corn meal. Roll out on floured surface to a 15x10-inch rectangle. Place on ungreased cookie sheet. Spread filling on half of dough, lengthwise, to within ½-inch of edge. Moisten edges; fold other half over to form rectangle. Seal edge with fork. Prick top crust for escape of steam. Bake at 425° for 25 to 30 minutes until golden brown. Serve with hot Sauce.

<u>Sauce</u>: Sauté mushrooms in butter. Add water and milk; blend in gravy mix. Cook over medium heat, stirring constantly until mixture boils. Boil 1 minute. Add pimiento.

The chicken pie to end all chicken pies. Frozen vegetables lend color, and the topping is buttered crumbs. Allow about an hour to make and bake.

Log Cabin Chicken Pie

1 cup Pillsbury's Best All Purpose Flour*
½ teaspoon salt
⅓ cup shortening
1 tablespoon lemon juice
2 to 3 tablespoons milk
½ cup chopped celery
¼ cup chopped green pepper
2 tablespoons butter
¾ cup water
1 package Pillsbury Chicken Gravy Mix
½ teaspoon salt
½ teaspoon poultry seasoning
⅛ teaspoon pepper
10-ounce package frozen peas and carrots,
    partially thawed
3 cups cubed cooked chicken
2 tablespoons butter, melted
½ cup dry bread crumbs

OVEN 400°   4 TO 6 SERVINGS

Combine flour and salt in mixing bowl. Cut in shortening until particles are fine. Sprinkle with lemon juice; mix. Add milk, stirring until dough holds together. Form into ball. Roll out on floured surface to fit a 9-inch pie pan. Fold edge to form a standing rim; flute. Sauté celery and green pepper in butter in large skillet. Blend in water, gravy mix, salt, poultry seasoning and pepper. Cook over medium heat, stirring constantly, until thickened. Stir in peas and carrots. Heat until vegetables are thawed. Stir in chicken. Spoon into pie shell. Blend together butter and bread crumbs; sprinkle over filling. Bake at 400° for 25 to 30 minutes, until golden brown.

*For use with Pillsbury's Best Self-Rising Flour, omit salt.

An unusual cream cheese tart, filled with bits of chicken, topped with almonds. This will take about an hour and a half.

MENU

Luncheon
Chicken Little Pies
Quick Tomato Aspic Salad
Fresh Fruit Platter
Beverage

Chicken Little Pies

3-ounce package cream cheese
I teaspoon chopped chives
¼ cup butter, softened
I cup Pillsbury's Best All Purpose Flour*
¼ teaspoon salt

Chicken Filling

4-ounce can mushroom stems and pieces, drained
⅓ cup chopped onion
2 tablespoons butter
2 cups cubed cooked chicken
10½-ounce can condensed cream of chicken soup
¼ teaspoon poultry seasoning
⅛ teaspoon pepper

Topping

I cup toasted bread cubes
¼ cup slivered almonds
2 tablespoons butter, melted

88

OVEN 425°   6 SERVINGS

Place cream cheese, chives and butter in small mixer bowl. Blend at low speed until creamy. Gradually add flour and salt, blending well. Mixture will be pilly. Form into a ball. Cover and chill while preparing Chicken Filling. Divide dough into 6 equal portions. Roll out each portion on floured surface to 6-inch circles. Fit loosely into 4-inch tart pans. Trim even with edge. Fill with Chicken Filling. Sprinkle with Topping. Place tarts on cookie sheet and bake at 425° for 25 to 30 minutes.

Chicken Filling: Saute mushrooms and onion in butter in a large skillet. Blend in chicken, soup, poultry seasoning and pepper.

Topping: Toss bread cubes and almonds with melted butter.

Tips: Omit pastry. Prepare filling as directed adding 1 package frozen green beans, cooked or a 1-pound can green beans. Place in a greased 1½-quart casserole. Sprinkle with Topping. Bake at 400° for 25 to 30 minutes.

A 3-ounce package of cream cheese with chives can be used in pastry instead of cream cheese and chives.

*For use with Pillsbury's Best Self-Rising Flour, omit salt.

Savory Chicken Bread Bake

I package active dry yeast
¼ cup warm water
½ cup milk, scalded
I tablespoon sugar
I teaspoon salt
I egg
2 cups Pillsbury's Best All Purpose Flour*
10½-ounce can condensed cream of
    mushroom soup
½ cup milk

Savory Chicken

½ cup chopped celery
½ cup chopped onion
4-ounce can mushroom stems and pieces,
    drained
¼ cup butter
3 cups cubed cooked chicken
I cup shredded Cheddar cheese
¼ cup chopped pimiento
I teaspoon poultry seasoning
½ teaspoon salt
⅛ teaspoon pepper

OVEN 400°   8 SERVINGS

Soften yeast in water. Combine milk, sugar and salt in mixing bowl. Cool to lukewarm. Add egg and yeast; mix well. Gradually add flour, mixing well, to form a soft dough. Cover. Let rise in warm place (85°-90°F.) until light and doubled, about 1½ hours. Add Savory Chicken to dough; mix well. Turn into greased 8 or 9-inch square baking dish. Cover, let rise until light and doubled in size, about 45 minutes. Bake at 400° for 20 to 25 minutes until golden brown. Serve with mushroom sauce prepared by combining soup and milk; heat thoroughly.

Savory Chicken: Sauté celery, onion and mushrooms in butter. Stir in remaining ingredients. Cool.

*For use with Pillsbury's Best Self-Rising Flour, omit salt.

HIGH ALTITUDE ADJUSTMENT — 5,200 FEET.
During first rising time, decrease rising time from 1½ hours to I hour.

Chicken Devil Puffs

I cup water
½ cup shortening
I cup Pillsbury's Best All Purpose Flour*
½ teaspoon salt
½ teaspoon dry mustard
4 eggs
4½-ounce can deviled ham

Chicken Filling

2 tablespoons butter or chicken fat
⅓ cup Pillsbury's Best All Purpose or
    Self-Rising Flour
½ teaspoon dry mustard
¼ teaspoon salt
1/16 teaspoon cayenne pepper
I cup milk or chicken broth
I cup light cream
3 cups cubed cooked chicken
I cup shredded cheese
¼ cup chopped pimiento, if desired
I tablespoon dried parsley flakes

OVEN 400°   12 SERVINGS

Combine water and shortening in saucepan. Bring to boil. Add flour, salt and mustard all at once. Cook and stir over medium heat until mixture leaves sides of pan. Remove from heat. Add eggs, one at a time, beating vigorously after each. Stir in ¼ cup (half the can) of deviled ham. Drop by rounded tablespoonfuls onto greased cookie sheet. Bake at 400° for 40 to 45 minutes until golden brown. Split and serve warm with Chicken Filling.

Chicken Filling: Melt butter in saucepan with remainder of deviled ham. Blend in flour, mustard, salt and cayenne pepper. Gradually add milk and cream. Cook over medium heat, stirring constantly until thickened. Stir in chicken, cheese, pimiento and parsley. Heat through.

*For use with Pillsbury's Best Self-Rising Flour, omit salt.

Chicken Salad Pie

- 1½ cups Pillsbury's Best All Purpose Flour*
- ½ teaspoon salt
- ½ cup shortening
- 5 to 6 tablespoons water
- ½ cup dairy sour cream
- ¼ cup mayonnaise
- Shredded American cheese, to sprinkle

Chicken Salad

- 2 cups cubed cooked chicken
- 1 cup shredded American cheese
- ½ cup blanched slivered almonds
- ½ cup chopped celery
- 9-ounce can crushed pineapple, drained
- ½ teaspoon salt
- ½ teaspoon paprika
- ½ cup mayonnaise

OVEN 450°   6 SERVINGS

Combine flour and salt in mixing bowl. Cut in shortening until particles are fine. Sprinkle water over mixture while tossing and stirring lightly with fork until dough is moist enough to hold together. Shape into ball; flatten to ½-inch thickness, smoothing edge. Roll out on floured surface. Cut into 6-inch circles. Place six 6-ounce custard cups upside down on baking sheet. Place pastry circles on each, mold over cup to fit by making 5 or 6 pleats around edge. Prick bottom with fork. Bake at 450° for 10 to 12 minutes until golden. Cool 10 minutes. Remove pastry shells from cups. Cool completely. Fill with Chicken Salad. Fold together sour cream and mayonnaise. Place teaspoonfuls on top of each salad. Sprinkle with additional cheese. Chill until served.

Chicken Salad: Combine all ingredients with mayonnaise.

*For use with Pillsbury's Best Self-Rising Flour, omit salt.

Chicken Party Pie

9-inch Baked Pastry Shell, see page 5

- 1 package lemon gelatin
- 1 cup boiling water
- ½ cup dairy sour cream
- ½ cup mayonnaise
- 2 teaspoons onion salt
- 2 tablespoons lemon juice
- 1 tablespoon Worcestershire sauce
- 1½ cups cubed cooked chicken
- ⅓ cup chopped green pepper
- ¼ cup chopped ripe olives
- 2 tablespoons chopped pimiento

6 SERVINGS

Dissolve gelatin in boiling water. Stir in sour cream and mayonnaise until well blended. (If necessary, use rotary beater and beat slightly to remove lumps. Do not beat to frothy stage.) Chill until thickened but not set (about 45 minutes). Add onion salt, lemon juice and Worcestershire sauce. Fold in chicken, green pepper, ripe olives and pimiento. Chill until mixture is thickened. Pour into Baked Pastry Shell. Garnish with strips of green pepper and pimiento, if desired. Chill until firm.

Tips: If desired, add 1 teaspoon poppy seed to flour or pie crust mix when preparing Pastry Shell.

Omit Pastry Shell, pour mixture into 8-inch square pan. Chill until firm. Cut in squares and serve on lettuce cups.

Super Casseroles For Groups

• Two is company but ten is a group, and here are noteworthy recipes designed to handle any such situation. From church suppers to youngsters' birthday parties, from teen meets to neighborhood brunches, you can choose a recipe that fits the feast and leave them gasping at your ingenuity. These are the crowd-pleasers, chosen for popular flavor-appeal and do-ahead ease.

Ground beef a la stroganoff, with a bumper crop of tasty potato puffs on top. Shortcuts let you make it in an hour. For the smaller group, see page 17

Potato Pan Burger For A Crowd

2 pounds lean ground beef
2 packages Pillsbury Brown Gravy Mix
10½-ounce can condensed cream of
   mushroom soup
1¼ cups water
2 tablespoons catsup
1½ cups dairy sour cream
   Paprika, if desired

<u>Potato Puff Topping</u>

1½ cups water
¼ cup butter
1½ teaspoons salt
½ cup milk
2 cups Pillsbury Hungry Jack Mashed
   Potato Flakes
1 egg
½ cup Pillsbury's Best All Purpose or
   Self-Rising Flour
2 teaspoons baking powder

OVEN 400°   10 TO 12 SERVINGS

Brown ground beef in large skillet, stirring occasionally. Drain off excess fat. Blend in gravy mix, soup, water and catsup. Simmer, covered, 10 minutes. Stir in sour cream. Pour into 3-quart casserole. Drop Potato Puff Topping by tablespoonfuls onto filling. Sprinkle with additional potato flakes and paprika. Bake at 400° for 25 to 30 minutes.

<u>Potato Puff Topping</u>: Heat water, butter and salt to boiling in saucepan. Remove from heat, add milk. Stir in potato flakes. Let set 1 minute until moisture is absorbed. Whip lightly with fork. Add egg; blend well. Stir in flour and baking powder.

MENU

Birthday Party
Funny Face Hamburgers
Fruit Gelatin Salad
Potato Chips
Ice Cream and Cake
Milk

Have you ever had a hamburger look right back at you and smile? These do. They're fun to make, fun to eat. Allow an hour and a quarter to shape and bake.

Funny Face Hamburgers

1 pound lean ground beef
¼ cup Pillsbury's Best All Purpose or
   Self-Rising Flour
2 tablespoons dried parsley flakes
2 tablespoons catsup
1 teaspoon salt
½ teaspoon onion salt
¼ teaspoon pepper
1 can Pillsbury Refrigerated Quick
   Parkerhouse Dinner Rolls
6 pimiento strips
12 raisins
2 tablespoons Pillsbury Hungry Jack
   Mashed Potato Flakes
2 teaspoons cooking oil
   Milk

OVEN 375°   6 SERVINGS

Combine ground beef, flour, parsley flakes, catsup, salt, onion salt and pepper. Shape into 6 patties. Open can; separate dough into 12 rolls. On ungreased cookie sheet press 6 folded Parkerhouse Rolls into 4-inch circles. Place meat patty in center of each. Press each of the 6 remaining Parkerhouse Rolls into a 4-inch circle. Stretch each over meat patty and pinch well to seal to bottom crust. For faces snip through crust with scissors or sharp knife for eyes and mouth. Place raisins in holes for eyes; pimiento strip for mouth. For hair combine potato flakes and oil. Brush each roll with milk; sprinkle with potato flakes (or use shredded cheese or corn flakes for hair). Bake at 375° for 25 to 30 minutes.

Funny Face Hamburgers

Pimiento and parsley add a festive "confetti" look to this delicious chicken casserole perfect for a group with make ahead ease. For the family, see recipe on page 78

Chicken Almond Party Bake For A Crowd

10½-ounce can condensed cream of
    mushroom soup
10½-ounce can condensed cream of chicken
    soup
  2 (7-ounce) cans mushroom stems and
    pieces, drained
  6 cups cubed cooked chicken
  ¾ cup white wine or chicken broth
  I cup blanched slivered almonds
  ½ cup chopped pimiento
  2 tablespoons dried parsley flakes
  I tablespoon instant minced onion
  I teaspoon salt

<u>Potato Topping</u>
  2 cups water
  ¼ cup butter
  I teaspoon salt
  ½ cup milk
  3 cups Pillsbury Hungry Jack Mashed
    Potato Flakes
  I egg

OVEN 375°   10 TO 12 SERVINGS

Combine soups, mushrooms, chicken, wine, ¾ cup almonds, pimiento, parsley, onion and salt in 3-quart baking dish. Drop Potato Topping by tablespoonfuls on filling. Sprinkle with remaining almonds. Bake at 375° for 50 to 60 minutes until golden brown.

<u>Potato Topping</u>: Heat water, butter and salt to boiling in saucepan. Remove from heat. Add milk, stir in potato flakes with fork just until moistened. Let stand until liquid is absorbed (about ½ minute). Add egg and blend well.

<u>Tip:</u> Make up to 12 hours ahead. Cover. Refrigerate. Bake at 375° for 60 to 70 minutes.

Corn meal steals the show from corned beef in this colorful dish that smacks of the Old Southwest. Mix and bake in about an hour.

Corn In The Cobbler

  I package Pillsbury Golden Corn Muffin
    Mix
  I cup Pillsbury's Best All Purpose or
    Self-Rising Flour
  I cup milk
  2 eggs
  I teaspoon instant minced onion
  2 cups shredded Cheddar cheese

<u>Topping</u>
  12-ounce can corned beef
  2 (8-ounce) cans tomato sauce
  ½ cup finely chopped green pepper
  2 tablespoons instant minced onion
  2 tablespoons Worcestershire sauce
  ½ teaspoon salt
  ¼ teaspoon pepper

OVEN 375°   6 TO 8 SERVINGS

In large mixing bowl combine muffin mix, flour, milk, eggs, onion and I cup shredded Cheddar cheese. Mix thoroughly. Spread in bottom of greased 13x9-inch baking dish. Spread with Topping. Sprinkle with I cup shredded Cheddar cheese. Bake at 375° for 25 to 30 minutes.

<u>Topping</u>: Combine corned beef, tomato sauce, green pepper, onion, Worcestershire sauce, salt and pepper. Mix thoroughly breaking up corned beef.

<u>Tip:</u> If desired, add 2 tablespoons brown sugar to Topping.

Dill-flavored pastry squares rest lightly on tiny meatballs in a tomato-vegetable sauce. One and a half hours to serving time. Turn to page 20 if your "crowd" is small.

Dill-flavored pastry squares rest lightly on tiny meatballs in a tomato-vegetable sauce. One and a half hours to serving time. Turn to page 20 if your "crowd" is small.

MENU

Church Luncheon
Chicken and Dressing Casserole
Buttered Peas and Carrots
Cranberry-Orange Gelatin Salad
Apple Crisp
Beverage

Swedish Meatball Dinner For A Crowd

     3 medium onions, sliced
     2 pounds lean ground beef
     2 eggs
     ¾ cup dry bread crumbs or cracker crumbs
     ½ cup milk
      I teaspoon salt
      I teaspoon basil
     ¼ teaspoon pepper
     2 (10¾-ounce) cans condensed tomato
        soup
     ¼ cup water
     2 teaspoons Worcestershire sauce

Pastry
     I½ cups Pillsbury's Best All Purpose Flour*
     2 tablespoons grated Parmesan cheese
      I teaspoon dried parsley flakes
     ½ teaspoon salt
     ¼ teaspoon dill seed
     ½ cup shortening
     5 to 6 tablespoons milk

OVEN 425°   IO TO I2 SERVINGS

Arrange onion slices on bottom of 13x9-inch baking dish. Combine ground beef, eggs, bread crumbs, milk, salt, basil and pepper. Shape into I-inch meatballs. Place on top of onion slices. Bake at 425° for 20 minutes. Remove from oven. Pour tomato soup, water and Worcestershire sauce over top. Stir carefully just to blend. Arrange Pastry on meat mixture. Sprinkle with additional Parmesan cheese. Bake at 425° for 30 to 35 minutes.

Pastry: Combine flour, Parmesan cheese, parsley, salt and dill seed in mixing bowl. Cut in shortening until particles are the size of small peas. Add milk and stir until dough clings together. Roll out on floured surface to a 13x9-inch rectangle. Cut into squares or triangles.

*For use with Pillsbury's Best Self-Rising Flour, omit salt.

Layers of chicken bites and dressing captured in custard, gilded with Parmesan cheese and almonds. Prepare in advance, to bake later and serve in quarters.

Chicken and Dressing Casserole

     5 cups toasted dry bread cubes
      I cup chopped celery
     3 cups cubed cooked chicken
      I tablespoon instant minced onion
     5 eggs
     2 (10½-ounce) cans condensed cream of
        chicken soup
     I½ cups milk
     I½ teaspoons salt
      I teaspoon poultry seasoning
     ⅛ teaspoon pepper
     ½ cup Pillsbury's Best All Purpose or
        Self-Rising Flour
     ¼ cup grated Parmesan cheese
     ¼ cup butter
     ½ cup blanched slivered almonds

OVEN 375°   IO TO I2 SERVINGS

Combine bread cubes and celery in greased 13x9-inch baking dish. Place chicken over bread cubes spreading to cover. Sprinkle with onion. Combine eggs, soup, milk, salt, poultry seasoning and pepper. Pour over chicken in casserole. Combine flour and Parmesan cheese. Cut in butter until crumbly. Sprinkle over casserole; then top with almonds. Bake at 375° for 35 to 40 minutes until knife inserted near center comes out clean.

Tip: This can be prepared ahead, covered and refrigerated. Bake at 375° for 45 to 50 minutes.

A picture-pretty baked stew, ringed with parsley dumplings. Allow two and a half hours or prepare ahead except for the dumplings.

Beef 'N Dumpling Bake

2 pounds stew meat, cut into I-inch cubes
2 medium onions, sliced
⅓ cup Pillsbury's Best All Purpose or
    Self-Rising Flour
I teaspoon salt
⅛ teaspoon pepper
10½-ounce can condensed golden mushroom
    soup
I cup water
I tablespoon Worcestershire sauce
I bay leaf
10-ounce package frozen green peas, thawed
4 green pepper rings

Parsley Dumplings
I cup Pillsbury's Best All Purpose Flour*
2 tablespoons dried parsley flakes
1½ teaspoons baking powder
½ teaspoon salt
¼ teaspoon sage
½ cup milk
2 tablespoons cooking oil
I egg

OVEN 350°   8 TO 10 SERVINGS

Place stew meat and onions in 3-quart casserole. Sprinkle with flour, salt and pepper. Toss lightly to coat meat. Bake uncovered at 350° for 30 minutes.

Stir in soup, water, Worcestershire sauce and bay leaf. Cover and bake at 350° for 2 hours. Remove bay leaf. Stir in peas. Arrange green pepper rings in center. Drop Parsley Dumplings by rounded teaspoonfuls around edge. Cover. Bake 20 minutes or until dumplings spring back when lightly touched.

Parsley Dumplings: Combine flour, parsley, baking powder, salt and sage in medium mixing bowl. Combine milk, oil and egg. Add to dry ingredients all at once, stirring only until dry particles are moistened.

Tip: To make ahead, prepare except for Parsley Dumplings. Cool, cover and refrigerate. When ready to bake, cover and place in oven 20 minutes before adding Parsley Dumplings.

*For use with Pillsbury's Best Self-Rising Flour, omit baking powder and salt.

Dumplings, biscuits or pastry can provide a new horizon on an attractive main dish.

Remember to add almonds or other nuts, once in awhile, to give a casserole good crunchy flavor.

Festive red cranberries and aromatic spices make this a holiday favorite. Ready for the gala affair in an hour and a half. See page 125 for the smaller size recipe.

Cranberry Whirl Ham Dinner For A Crowd

6 cups cubed cooked ham
6 cups sliced cooked sweet potatoes
I-pound 14-ounce can pineapple chunks,
    drained, reserving juice
I-pound can whole cranberry sauce
¾ cup firmly packed brown sugar
3 tablespoons flour
I teaspoon cinnamon
¼ teaspoon ground cloves

OVEN 375°   12 SERVINGS

Place half of ham, sweet potatoes and pineapple chunks in layers in 3-quart casserole. Spoon half of cranberry sauce, by teaspoonfuls over casserole. Repeat layers. Combine ¼ cup brown sugar, flour, cinnamon and cloves in small saucepan. Blend in I cup reserved pineapple juice. Cook over medium heat until mixture boils. Drizzle over mixture in casserole. Sprinkle with ½ cup brown sugar. Bake uncovered at 375° for 45 to 50 minutes.

Tip: Two I-pound I-ounce vacuum pack cans of sweet potatoes yields 6 cups.

It's bacon and eggs, ham and cheese, baked on a crust and served in strips. Ready in an hour and a half. For a smaller Brunch Pizza, see page 47

Brunch Pizza For A Crowd

1½ cups Pillsbury's Best All Purpose Flour*
¼ teaspoon salt
⅛ teaspoon pepper
½ cup shortening
5 to 6 tablespoons water
1 pound sliced bacon
8 slices cooked ham
8-ounces sliced Swiss cheese
4 eggs, slightly beaten
1¼ cups milk
¼ teaspoon salt

OVEN 425°   10 TO 12 SERVINGS

Combine flour, salt and pepper in mixing bowl. Cut in shortening until particles are fine. Sprinkle water over mixture while stirring with fork until dough holds together. Form into a square. Flatten to ½-inch thickness; smooth edges. Roll out on a floured surface to a 15x10-inch rectangle. Fit loosely into a 13x9-inch pan.

Fry bacon until crisp. Drain on absorbent paper; crumble. Place ham slices on bottom of pastry lined pan. Top with cheese slices, then with bacon. Combine eggs, milk and salt; pour carefully over bacon. Bake at 425° for 20 to 25 minutes until lightly browned and set. Cool 5 to 10 minutes before cutting and serving.

<u>Tip:</u> If desired, prepare crust ahead, fit into pan, add ham, cheese and bacon. Cover tightly and refrigerate. Just before baking add egg and milk mixture. Increase baking time about 5 minutes.

*For use with Pillsbury's Best Self-Rising Flour, omit salt.

Creole Gumbo For A Crowd

2 cups sliced celery
I cup chopped onion
I cup chopped green pepper
3 cloves minced garlic
¼ cup olive or cooking oil
¼ cup Pillsbury's Best All Purpose or
    Self-Rising Flour
I-pound 12-ounce can tomatoes
15-ounce can tomato sauce
2 tablespoons Worcestershire sauce
4 teaspoons salt
I-pound can okra, undrained
12-ounce package frozen shrimp, partially
    thawed
2 (6-ounce) packages frozen crabmeat,
    partially thawed
½ cup cooking sherry
2 tablespoons dried parsley flakes

Cheesy Quick Croutons
2 cans Pillsbury Refrigerated Hungry Jack
    Flaky or Flaky Buttermilk Biscuits
    Milk
½ cup grated Parmesan cheese
¼ cup corn meal

Cheesy-quick croutons accompany this crowd-sized Southern gumbo. Ready and steaming in one hour and forty-five minutes. See page 126 for smaller recipe.

OVEN 400°   12 SERVINGS

Sauté celery, onion, green pepper and garlic in oil in 6-quart Dutch oven until tender, about 10 minutes. Stir in flour; blend in tomatoes, tomato sauce, Worcestershire sauce and salt. Cover and simmer for 45 minutes to 1 hour. Add okra, shrimp, crabmeat, sherry and parsley.

Simmer for 20 minutes, stirring occasionally. Serve in bowls with Cheesy Quick Croutons.

Cheesy Quick Croutons: Unroll dough; separate into 20 biscuits. Cut biscuits in quarters. Dip in milk, then roll in mixture of Parmesan cheese and corn meal. Place on two baking sheets. Bake at 400° for 8 to 10 minutes until golden brown.

Eggs and Canadian bacon are set like jewels in a foundation of sour cream hash brown potatoes . . . baked and beautiful in an hour and a half. For the family, see page 66.

Gold Rush Brunch For A Crowd

 1 package Pillsbury Hash Brown Potatoes
½ cup chopped onion
 2 tablespoons dried parsley flakes
¼ cup butter
½ cup Pillsbury's Best All Purpose Flour*
 1 teaspoon salt
¼ teaspoon pepper
1½ cups milk
 1 cup dairy sour cream
 1 to 1½ pounds (16 slices) sliced
    Canadian style bacon
 8 eggs

OVEN 350°   8 SERVINGS

Prepare potatoes according to package directions; drain well. Stir in onion and parsley. Place in greased 13x9-inch baking dish. Melt butter in saucepan; blend in flour, salt and pepper. Add milk. Cook over low heat, stirring constantly, until thickened. Remove from heat, blend in sour cream. Pour over potatoes, lifting potatoes lightly to permit sauce to mix well. Arrange bacon in an overlapping row down center of dish. Bake at 350° for 45 minutes. Remove from oven. Make 4 indentations on each side of bacon; slip 1 egg carefully into each indentation. Season with salt and pepper as desired. Bake 15 to 20 minutes longer or until eggs are set.

Tip: Potato and sauce mixture can be made ahead of time, covered and refrigerated. Add bacon just before placing in oven and bake an additional 5 minutes.

*For use with Pillsbury's Best Self-Rising Flour, omit salt.

MENU

Shower Brunch Buffet
Gold Rush Brunch
Assorted Sweet Rolls
Fresh Fruits in Watermelon Half
Beverage

Instant minced onion or garlic can be substituted nicely for the "fresh chopped" ingredient.

Cut fresh vegetables in a variety of sizes and shapes for interest.

Many main dishes can be prepared early in the day and refrigerated until time to tuck in the oven to heat through and brown just before serving.

This is a leavened pastry, like a giant bun with the seasoned meat baked inside. Serve in juicy pie-shaped wedges. Easy to make in a little over an hour.

Burger For A Bunch

Crust

2 cups Pillsbury's Best All Purpose Flour*
I tablespoon sugar
I teaspoon salt
I teaspoon soda
I teaspoon cream of tartar
⅔ cup shortening
½ cup milk

Filling

I pound lean ground beef
½ cup Pillsbury Hungry Jack Mashed
   Potato Flakes or cracker crumbs
⅓ cup catsup
2 tablespoons instant minced onion
2 tablespoons pickle relish
I tablespoon prepared mustard
I egg
½ cup shredded cheese

Potato Flake Topping

3 tablespoons Pillsbury Hungry Jack
   Mashed Potato Flakes
I tablespoon cooking oil
¼ teaspoon salt

OVEN 375°   8 TO 10 SERVINGS

Mix together flour, sugar, salt, soda and cream of tartar in mixing bowl. Cut in shortening until mixture resembles coarse crumbs. Stir in milk until dough clings together. Divide in half. Roll out one half to a 9-inch circle on slightly floured surface. Place on ungreased cookie sheet. Roll out remaining dough to a 10-inch circle. Spread Filling to within ½-inch of edge of crust on cookie sheet. Sprinkle with cheese. Place 10-inch circle on top of Filling. Moisten edges and seal. Brush top with milk. Sprinkle Potato Flake Topping over burger. Bake at 375° for 35 to 40 minutes.

Filling: Combine ground beef and other ingredients except cheese.

Potato Flake Topping: Combine potato flakes, oil and salt.

Tips: Burger may be made ahead of time. Cover. Place in refrigerator several hours or overnight. Bake at 375° for 40 to 45 minutes.

Crust may be made with Pillsbury Butterflake Recipe Pie Crust Mix adding I tablespoon sugar, I teaspoon cream of tartar, I teaspoon soda and ⅓ cup milk.

Sesame seed may be substituted for Potato Flake Topping.

*For use with Pillsbury's Best Self-Rising Flour, omit salt and decrease soda to ¼ teaspoon.

A popular casserole for a large crowd; complete in about an hour and a quarter. For a smaller casserole, see page 14.

Crowd Size Hungry Boys' Casserole

   I cup chopped celery
½ cup chopped onion
½ cup chopped green pepper
   I small clove garlic, minced
   2 pounds lean ground beef
   I-pound can pork and beans
   15-ounce can garbanzo beans
   8-ounce can tomato sauce
½ cup sliced stuffed olives, if desired
¼ cup catsup
¼ cup water
1½ teaspoons salt
½ cup blanched slivered almonds

Biscuits
   2 cups Pillsbury's Best All Purpose Flour*
   3 teaspoons baking powder
   I teaspoon salt
⅔ cup milk
⅓ cup cooking oil
   8 drops yellow food coloring

OVEN 425°   10 TO 12 SERVINGS

Sprinkle celery, onion, green pepper and garlic in 13x9-inch baking dish or 3-quart casserole. Crumble ground beef on top. Bake uncovered at 425° for 20 minutes. Remove from oven. Stir in beans, tomato sauce, olives, catsup, water and salt until well blended. Reserve 1 cup of bean-meat mixture. Return casserole to oven for 15 minutes while preparing Biscuits. Arrange Biscuits without centers on casserole. Spoon reserved bean-meat mixture in hole of each Biscuit. Sprinkle casserole with almonds. Top with biscuit holes. Bake at 425° for 15 to 20 minutes until golden.

Biscuits: Combine flour, baking powder and salt in mixing bowl. Combine milk, oil and food coloring. Add to dry ingredients all at once stirring until dough clings together. Knead on floured surface 10 times. Roll out to ¼-inch thickness. Cut with doughnut cutter, saving holes.

*For use with Pillsbury's Best Self-Rising Flour, omit baking powder and salt.

This will bring out the artist in you, and draw a smile from every guest. A natural for children's birthday parties. Just forty-five minutes to serve your "catch".

Seafood Sunfish

   6½-ounce can tuna, drained
   I cup shredded American cheese
   2 tablespoons pickle relish
   2 cans Pillsbury Refrigerated Hungry Jack
      Flaky or Flaky Buttermilk Biscuits
      Sliced stuffed olives

OVEN 375°   7 SERVINGS

Combine tuna, cheese and pickle relish. Unroll dough from 2 cans; separate into 20 biscuits. Press 7 biscuits into 5-inch circles on ungreased cookie sheet. Cut 6 biscuits in quarters. Arrange 3 of the quarters on each circle for the fins and tail; flatten. Place a heaping tablespoonful of tuna filling on center of each. Press 7 remaining biscuits into 5-inch circles. Place over filling, stretching to seal edges. Pinch a "U" shape for mouth on side opposite tail. Press sliced olive slightly into dough for eye. With scissors, clip body for "scales"; clip fins and tails. Bake at 375° for 12 to 15 minutes.

Don't overlook the many varieties of cheeses to add their distinctive flavor!

More toppings to try on your next casserole could include chopped nuts or crisp bacon.

Cheese goes over and under the savory sausage-and-tomato sauce, lovingly layered on a yeast dough rectangle. Ready for double enjoyment in ninety minutes.

MENU

Mid-Night Supper
Double Pizza Special
Tossed Salad with Italian Dressing
Relishes
Spumoni Ice Cream
Beverage

Double Pizza Special

Meat Sauce

I pound pork sausage
¼ cup chopped onion
I clove garlic, minced
I-pound can tomatoes
6-ounce can tomato paste
4-ounce can mushroom stems and pieces,
   drained
I teaspoon oregano
I teaspoon salt
⅛ teaspoon pepper

Crust

I package active dry yeast
½ cup warm water
I½ teaspoons sugar
½ teaspoon salt
I tablespoon cooking oil
I¼ to I½ cups Pillsbury's Best All Purpose
   Flour*

Cheese Filling

- 1 egg, slightly beaten
- 1 cup (¼ pound) shredded Mozzarella cheese
- 1 pound dry cottage cheese or ricotta cheese
- ¼ cup dried parsley flakes
- ½ teaspoon salt

Topping

- 2 cups (½ pound) shredded Mozzarella cheese
- ½ teaspoon oregano
- ¼ cup grated Parmesan cheese

OVEN 425°   10 TO 12 SERVINGS

Brown sausage with onion and garlic in large skillet. Drain off fat. Add tomatoes, tomato paste, mushrooms, oregano, salt and pepper. Simmer 15 minutes. Cool to lukewarm. While Meat Sauce is cooking prepare Crust and Cheese Filling. Pat Crust over bottom of greased 15x10-inch jelly roll pan. Spread with Cheese Filling and then Meat Sauce. Bake at 425° on lowest shelf for 20 minutes; remove from oven and sprinkle with Mozzarella cheese, then oregano and Parmesan cheese. Bake for an additional 10 to 15 minutes until golden brown.

Crust: Soften yeast in warm water in mixing bowl. Add sugar, salt and oil; mix well. Gradually add flour to form a stiff dough. Knead on floured surface just until smooth; about 2 minutes. Let dough rest 10 minutes on greased 15x10-inch jelly roll pan.

Cheese Filling: Combine egg, Mozzarella cheese, dry cottage or ricotta cheese, parsley and salt. Mix well.

Tip: Grease tips of fingers for easier handling of dough when patting into pan.

*For use with Pillsbury's Best Self-Rising Flour, omit salt.

"Ultra"
Casseroles
For Company

● Set a mood with food: spices that tell of distant places, the delicate aroma of cooking wines that whet the appetite, the offbeat vegetables that create excitement on the menu . . . these are the makings of gourmet cookery. In this chapter, we offer new twists on old world favorites, exotic oriental dishes, and out-of-the-ordinary seafood specials.

A rare rarebit is this, hiding flavorful chunks of crabmeat and topped with tiny poppy-seed biscuits. Ready in an hour.

Crabmeat Cobbler

  ½ cup chopped green pepper
  ½ cup chopped onion
  ¼ cup butter
  ¼ cup flour
    I teaspoon dry mustard
    I-pound can tomatoes
    I tablespoon Worcestershire sauce
   6-ounce package frozen crabmeat,
     partially thawed
    I cup shredded American cheese
  ¼ cup cooking sherry
    I teaspoon poppy seed

Biscuit Topping

    I cup Pillsbury's Best All Purpose Flour*
   2 teaspoons baking powder
  ½ teaspoon salt
  ½ cup shredded American cheese
  ½ cup milk
   2 tablespoons cooking oil

OVEN 425°   6 SERVINGS

Sauté green pepper and onion in butter in saucepan until tender, about 5 minutes. Blend in flour and mustard. Gradually stir in tomatoes and Worcestershire sauce. Cook over medium heat until mixture boils and thickens. Add crabmeat; simmer, covered, 10 minutes. Stir in cheese and sherry. Pour into 1½-quart casserole. Drop Biscuit Topping by teaspoonfuls on crabmeat mixture. Sprinkle with poppy seed. Bake at 425° for 15 to 20 minutes.

Biscuit Topping: Combine flour, baking powder, salt and cheese in mixing bowl. Add milk and oil all at once, stirring only until moistened.

Tip: For a quick topping, use I can Pillsbury Refrigerated Flaky Tenderflake or Flaky Tenderflake Buttermilk Biscuits. Place filling in a 2-quart casserole. Open can; separate dough into 12 biscuits. Cut each biscuit in quarters. Arrange on casserole with point up. Sprinkle with poppy seed. Bake at 375° for 20 to 25 minutes.

*For use with Pillsbury's Best Self-Rising Flour, omit baking powder and salt.

Tater tots set sail in a wine seasoned mixture of shrimp, peas and onions. You can set supper in forty-five minutes.

Shrimp Boat Supper

10½-ounce can condensed cream of
    mushroom soup
   I-pound I-ounce can peas and onions,
    drained
   7-ounce package frozen shrimp, broken
    apart
  ¼ cup white cooking wine
 1/16 teaspoon hot pepper sauce
   I-pound package frozen tater tots

OVEN 425°   4 TO 5 SERVINGS

Combine soup, peas and onions, shrimp, wine and hot pepper sauce in 8-inch square baking dish. Arrange tater tots over top. Bake at 425° for 25 to 30 minutes until golden brown and bubbly.

Crabmeat Cobbler

A do-ahead seafood special, with the textury treasures of green beans and almonds. Ready for seafood lovers in less than an hour.

Crab 'N Clam Crisp

7½-ounce can crabmeat, drained
  8-ounce can minced clams, drained
  1-pound can French cut green beans,
    drained
  1 cup chopped celery
  1 tablespoon flour
  1 teaspoon instant minced onion
  ½ cup mayonnaise
  ¼ cup diced roasted almonds
  2 tablespoons corn flake crumbs
  2 tablespoons grated Parmesan cheese
  2 tablespoons diced roasted almonds

OVEN 350°   4 TO 5 SERVINGS

Combine crabmeat, clams, beans, celery, flour and onion in mixing bowl. Stir in mayonnaise and ¼ cup almonds. Place in 1½-quart casserole. Sprinkle with corn flake crumbs, Parmesan cheese and 2 tablespoons almonds. Bake at 350° for 30 to 35 minutes.

Tip: Prepare ahead, cover and refrigerate. Bake as directed.

Picture pretty pink salmon and bright green peas accented with bits of ripe olive. You can top patty shells with this in thirty minutes.

Salmon-In-A-Shell

  ¼ cup butter
  ¼ cup Pillsbury's Best All Purpose or
    Self-Rising Flour
1¾ cups milk
  ¼ teaspoon salt
  ½ cup shredded Cheddar cheese
  1-pound can salmon, drained and flaked
10-ounce package frozen peas, partially
    thawed
  ⅓ cup chopped ripe olives, if desired
  2 tablespoons cooking sherry, if desired
  6 to 8 baked patty shells

            6 TO 8 SERVINGS

Melt butter in medium saucepan. Blend in flour. Gradually add milk. Cook over medium heat, stirring constantly, until thickened. Add salt, cheese, salmon, peas, olives and cooking sherry. Simmer, covered, for 15 to 20 minutes. Serve over patty shells.

The pasta family with its many shapes of macaroni, spaghetti and noodles provide the main ingredient for several casserole dishes.

For color in a party main dish you might use green pepper, pimiento, parsley flakes or hard-cooked eggs.

A crater of hot rice, filled with chunky chicken and ham, crowned with mandarin oranges. An easy-do recipe that takes but thirty minutes or so.

Chicken Delish

2 cups diced cooked chicken
I cup diced cooked ham
4-ounce can mushroom stems and pieces, drained
10½-ounce can condensed cream of chicken soup
½ cup milk
½ cup diced roasted almonds
¼ to ½ teaspoon nutmeg
⅛ teaspoon allspice
⅛ teaspoon pepper
4 cups cooked rice
4 teaspoons dried parsley flakes
II-ounce can mandarin oranges, drained

4 TO 6 SERVINGS

Combine chicken, ham, mushrooms, cream of chicken soup, milk, almonds, nutmeg, allspice and pepper in a large saucepan. Bring to boil; cover and simmer over low heat for 10 to 15 minutes. Prepare rice as directed on package. When cooked, add parsley flakes. To serve, place rice on a large platter. Make a large indentation in center. Fill with chicken filling and garnish with mandarin oranges.

Tip: Use extra mandarin oranges in a salad or as topping for pudding.

These colorful wedges make an extraordinary vegetable side dish with an Italian accent. Start with the pastry shell about an hour and a half before serving time.

Cheesy Eggplant Pie

9-inch Unbaked Pastry Shell, see page 5
¼ cup chopped green pepper
¼ cup chopped onion
¼ cup butter
8-ounce can tomato sauce
½ teaspoon salt
3 cups sliced and quartered eggplant
2 cups shredded Cheddar or Mozzarella cheese

OVEN 400°   5 TO 6 SERVINGS

Saute´ green pepper and onion in butter in medium skillet until tender. Blend in tomato sauce and salt. Bring to boil. Add eggplant. Cook, stirring occasionally, 10 minutes until eggplant is almost tender. Place half of eggplant mixture in Unbaked Pastry Shell. Top with half of cheese. Add remainder of eggplant, then sprinkle remainder of cheese over top. Bake at 400° for 30 to 35 minutes. Let stand 10 minutes before cutting in wedges and serving.

Tip: Prepare ahead, cover and refrigerate. Bake at 400° for 45 minutes.

Soufflés collapse quickly when exposed to room temperature, so have everything ready before removing from the oven.

Under the golden soufflé is a savory mixture of veal and herbs. Serve hot from the oven in an hour and a half.

Top Hat Veal Pie

9-inch Unbaked Pastry Shell, see page 5

> I pound ground veal
> 2 tablespoons shortening
> I tablespoon instant minced onion
> I to 2 bay leaves
> I cup water
> I tablespoon flour
> I tablespoon dried parsley flakes
> I teaspoon salt
> ⅛ teaspoon pepper
> ¹⁄₁₆ teaspoon thyme
> ¹⁄₁₆ teaspoon ginger
> I egg, slightly beaten

Cheese Soufflé

> 2 tablespoons butter
> 2 tablespoons flour
> ½ cup milk
> I cup shredded Cheddar cheese
> 2 eggs, separated

OVEN 425°   5 TO 6 SERVINGS

Brown ground veal in shortening in large skillet. Add onion, bay leaf and water. Simmer uncovered for I5 minutes, stirring occasionally. Stir in flour, parsley, salt, pepper, thyme, ginger and egg. Pour into Unbaked Pastry Shell. Bake at 425° for I5 minutes while preparing Cheese Soufflé. Reduce oven temperature to 375°. Pour Soufflé over partially baked pie, sealing to edge of crust. Bake at 375° for 20 to 25 minutes.

Cheese Soufflé: Melt butter in medium saucepan. Blend in flour. Gradually add milk. Cook over medium heat, stirring constantly, until thickened. Add cheese, stir until melted. Remove from heat. Add egg yolks. Blend in thoroughly. Beat egg whites until stiff, but not dry. Gently fold into cheese mixture.

A tuna soufflé gone high-hat with curry and almonds, olives and a hint of sherry. Time it to a "T", at about an hour and a half.

Tuna Triumph

　¼ cup butter
　⅓ cup Pillsbury's Best All Purpose
　　or Self-Rising Flour
　1 teaspoon salt
　½ teaspoon Worcestershire sauce
　¼ teaspoon curry powder
　　Dash hot pepper sauce
　1¼ cups milk
　4 eggs, separated
　¼ cup cooking sherry
　6½-ounce can tuna, drained
　¼ cup chopped ripe olives
　2 tablespoons chopped pimiento
　¼ cup slivered almonds

OVEN 350°　　　　　　　　　6 SERVINGS

Melt butter in large saucepan. Blend in flour, salt, Worcestershire sauce, curry and hot pepper sauce. Gradually add milk, stirring until smooth. Cook over medium heat, stirring constantly, until mixture boils. Blend mixture into slightly beaten egg yolks. Return to saucepan and cook over medium heat until thick and mixture loses gloss. Blend in sherry. Stir in tuna, olives and pimiento. Beat egg whites until stiff but not dry. Fold into seafood mixture. Pour into ungreased 1½-quart casserole or soufflé dish. Sprinkle with almonds. Place in pan with at least 1-inch hot water. Bake at 350° for 50 to 55 minutes until a knife inserted near center comes out clean. Serve immediately.

HIGH ALTITUDE ADJUSTMENT — 5,200 FEET. Bake at 350° for 65 to 70 minutes.

A casserole creole you can make in an hour and serve with the rice over or under. An easy do-ahead dish.

Louisiana Shrimp Bake

　1 cup sliced celery
　1 medium sliced onion
　½ cup chopped green pepper
　¼ cup butter
　¼ cup Pillsbury's Best All Purpose
　　or Self-Rising Flour
　1½ teaspoons salt
　　1-pound can tomatoes
　　7-ounce package frozen shrimp
　¼ cup cooking sherry
　1½ cups shredded Cheddar cheese
　4 hard-cooked eggs, sliced
　3 cups cooked rice

OVEN 375°　　　　　　6 TO 8 SERVINGS

Sauté celery, onion and green pepper in butter in medium saucepan, about 5 minutes. Blend in flour and salt; cook until bubbly. Stir in tomatoes, shrimp and sherry. Bring to boil; simmer covered for 10 minutes. Stir in ½ cup cheese and eggs. Pour into 2-quart casserole. Top with rice; sprinkle with remaining 1 cup cheese. Bake at 375° for 25 to 30 minutes.

Tips: Prepare ahead, cool, cover and refrigerate. Bake at 375° for 35 to 40 minutes.

For quick main dish, add all of cheese to shrimp mixture. Heat through. Serve over rice.

Louisiana Shrimp Bake

During the first baking period for your main dishes, prepare the remaining ingredients and toppings that will be added later.

Reminiscent of the pepper steak of the Far East, finished off with mustardy muffins on top. A one and a half hour masterpiece.

Steak Bake Casserole

1½ pounds cube or sirloin steak, cut in
  narrow strips
⅓ cup Pillsbury's Best All Purpose or
  Self-Rising Flour
1 teaspoon salt
¼ teaspoon pepper
1 onion, sliced
1 green pepper, sliced
1-pound can tomatoes
4-ounce can mushroom stems and pieces,
  drained
3 tablespoons molasses
3 tablespoons soy sauce
10-ounce package frozen French-cut beans,
  thawed and drained*
1 tablespoon sesame seed

Tangy Muffins

1¼ cups Pillsbury's Best All Purpose Flour**
1 ½ teaspoons baking powder
1 teaspoon dry mustard
½ teaspoon salt
½ cup milk
2 tablespoons cooking oil
1 egg

OVEN 400°   6 TO 8 SERVINGS

Place meat in 2½-quart casserole. Sprinkle with flour, salt and pepper. Toss to coat meat. Bake uncovered at 400° for 20 minutes.

Add onion, green pepper, tomatoes, mushrooms, molasses and soy sauce; mix well. Cover and bake at 400° for 30 minutes.

Stir in beans. Drop Tangy Muffins by tablespoonfuls onto hot meat mixture, sprinkle with sesame seed. Bake at 400° for 15 to 18 minutes.

Tangy Muffins: Combine flour, baking powder, dry mustard and salt in mixing bowl. Combine milk, oil and egg; add to dry ingredients all at once stirring until dry particles are moistened.

*Or use 1-pound can French-cut green beans, drained.

**For use with Pillsbury's Best Self-Rising Flour, omit baking powder and salt.

A new look to Yorkshire pudding, with a cheese accent. An accompaniment for your roast that will raise eyebrows and appetites. Start fifty minutes ahead.

Yorkshire Cheese Puff

2 tablespoons butter
1 cup Pillsbury's Best All Purpose Flour*
½ teaspoon salt
1/16 teaspoon pepper
2 eggs
1 cup milk
1 cup shredded American cheese

OVEN 400°   4 TO 6 SERVINGS

Melt butter in 9-inch square pan. Combine in mixer bowl flour, salt, pepper, eggs and milk. Beat with electric mixer or rotary beater until smooth. Stir in ½ cup cheese. Pour batter into 9-inch square pan. Sprinkle with remaining cheese. Bake at 400° for 30 to 35 minutes. Cut into serving pieces and serve hot with roasts or chicken.

*For use with Pillsbury's Best Self-Rising Flour, omit salt.

Steak Bake Casserole

Party Pork Barbecue

    I pound pork shoulder, cut in I-inch cubes
    ¼ cup Pillsbury's Best All Purpose or
        Self-Rising Flour
    1½ teaspoons salt
    ⅛ teaspoon pepper
    2 tablespoons cooking oil
    I cup sliced celery
    I medium green pepper, cut in 2-inch thin
        strips
    I small onion, sliced
    13½-ounce can pineapple tidbits, undrained
    ¾ cup catsup
    I tablespoon prepared mustard
    I tablespoon Worcestershire sauce
    4 cups cooked rice

Coated pork bites come to dinner in a sweet and tangy sauce over rice. Party time: in about forty-five minutes.

5 TO 6 SERVINGS

Coat pork with a mixture of flour, salt and pepper. Brown in oil in large skillet, using all the flour. Add celery, green pepper, onion, pineapple, catsup, mustard and Worcestershire sauce. Simmer, covered, 30 minutes. Serve over rice.

Tip: To keep warm, put rice in ovenproof dish or casserole, pushing rice up around edges. Pour barbecue-pork mixture in center. Place in warm oven for up to 30 minutes.

Delicious zucchini slices hidden under an airy bonnet of cheese puff. Allow an hour and a half for this, and serve promptly.

Zucchini Cheese Puff

   3 cups thinly sliced zucchini
   2 tablespoons flour
   ½ teaspoon salt
  1½ cups shredded Swiss cheese
   ¾ cup dairy sour cream
   2 eggs, separated
   ¼ cup plus 1 tablespoon dry bread crumbs
   1 tablespoon chopped chives
   ⅛ teaspoon pepper
   ¼ teaspoon cream of tartar
   2 tablespoons grated Parmesan cheese

OVEN 350°   5 TO 6 SERVINGS

Place zucchini in ungreased 1½-quart casserole. Sprinkle with flour, ¼ teaspoon salt and 1 cup Swiss cheese. Combine sour cream and egg yolks in mixing bowl. Mix in ¼ cup bread crumbs, chives, ¼ teaspoon salt and pepper. Beat egg whites with cream of tartar until stiff but not dry. Fold into sour cream mixture. Pour over zucchini. Sprinkle with remaining ½ cup Swiss cheese, 1 tablespoon bread crumbs and Parmesan cheese. Bake at 350° for 45 to 50 minutes.

Corned beef and mushrooms fill these individual rolls. Preparation and baking time takes only forty-five minutes with refrigerated dough as an easy base.

Corned Beef Wheels

 12-ounce can corned beef, finely chopped
  4-ounce can mushroom stems and pieces,
    drained and chopped
10½-ounce can condensed tomato soup
  1 can Pillsbury Refrigerated Quick Crescent
    Dinner Rolls
  ½ teaspoon caraway seed, if desired

Sauce
  2 tablespoons milk
  ¼ teaspoon salt
  ⅛ teaspoon pepper
  ½ cup dairy sour cream

OVEN 350°   6 TO 8 SERVINGS

Chop corned beef, add mushrooms and ⅓ cup tomato soup. Blend well. Open can; unroll dough, leaving together as 1 large rectangle. Press dough together at perforations and seams to form a 12x7-inch rectangle. Spread about 1½ cups of meat filling over dough. Starting with 12-inch side roll up dough jelly roll fashion, seal edges. Cut into 8 slices and place cut side down in greased muffin cups. Bake at 350° for 30 to 35 minutes. Let stand in muffin cups about 5 minutes before removing. Serve hot with Sauce.

Sauce: Combine remaining tomato soup, milk, salt, pepper and remaining meat mixture in a saucepan. Bring to boil. Stir in sour cream; heat, but do not boil.

Beautiful boned chicken breasts tucked among bright carrots and broccoli, enhanced with white wine, and a sour cream sauce. Plan one and three quarters hours to prepare.

Chicken A La Special

8 boned chicken breasts
1½ teaspoons salt
⅛ teaspoon pepper
¼ cup butter
½ cup white cooking wine
4 medium carrots, cut in 2-inch sticks

1 package frozen broccoli spears, cooked and drained
10½-ounce can condensed cream of chicken soup
2 tablespoons flour
4-ounce can mushroom stems and pieces, drained
½ cup dairy sour cream

Bone and remove skin from the chicken breasts. Sprinkle with salt and pepper. Melt butter in large skillet. Sauté chicken until golden brown, about 15 to 20 minutes, turning occasionally. Pour wine over chicken. Add carrot sticks, lifting chicken so the chicken is on top of carrots. Cover and steam for 50 to 60 minutes or until chicken and carrots are tender. Ten minutes before chicken is done, cook broccoli according to package directions. Drain. Remove chicken to a warm platter or serving casserole. Arrange carrots and broccoli alternately over chicken. Keep warm.

Blend cream of chicken soup, flour and mushrooms in a bowl. Add to liquid in skillet. Cook over medium heat until mixture has simmered for 3 to 4 minutes. Blend in sour cream and heat, but do not boil. Pour over chicken and vegetables. Serve hot.

Tip: To keep warm, cover chicken and vegetables and place in a 250° oven up to half an hour. Add hot sauce just before serving.

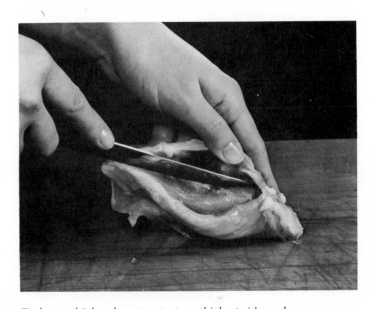

To bone chicken breasts, start on thickest side and cut along bone to release meat.

Tiny parsley biscuits top this delicious layered dish of spinach and mushroomed crab. You can call your guests in about sixty minutes.

Seafood Fantasy

10-ounce package frozen chopped spinach
10½-ounce can condensed cream of
    mushroom soup
¼ cup flour
½ cup milk
4-ounce can mushroom stems and pieces,
    drained
1 cup shredded Swiss cheese
2 (7½-ounce) cans crabmeat, drained and
    flaked
¼ cup diced roasted almonds
¼ cup white cooking wine

Parsley Biscuits
1 cup Pillsbury's Best All Purpose Flour*
1½ teaspoons sugar
1½ teaspoons baking powder
½ teaspoon salt
¼ cup butter
1 teaspoon dried parsley flakes
⅓ cup light cream
1 egg

OVEN 400°　　　　　　　4 TO 6 SERVINGS

Cook spinach as directed on package; drain well. Spread over bottom of 8-inch square baking dish or 2-quart casserole. Combine mushroom soup, flour, milk and mushrooms in a saucepan. Cook over medium heat until thickened. Add cheese, stir until melted. Stir in crabmeat, almonds and cooking wine. Pour over spinach in baking dish. Prepare Parsley Biscuits. Drop by teaspoonfuls over filling. Bake at 400° for 25 to 30 minutes until golden brown.

Parsley Biscuits: Combine flour, sugar, baking powder and salt in mixing bowl. Cut in butter until particles are fine. Stir in parsley, cream and egg until dough clings together.

Tips: If desired, omit cooking wine and increase milk ¼ cup.

If desired, omit Parsley Biscuits. Top with 1½ cups dry bread cubes combined with 3 tablespoons melted butter. Bake at 400° for 25 to 30 minutes.

*For use with Pillsbury's Best Self-Rising Flour, omit baking powder and salt.

For indoor clam bakes where you dig no further than your cupboard and freezer. A savory one hour get-together of prepared foods, topped with tender cream biscuits.

Easy Does It Clam Bake

10-ounce package frozen peas in butter
    sauce
9-ounce package frozen onions in cream
    sauce
½ cup milk
7½-ounce can minced clams, drained

Biscuits
1 cup Pillsbury's Best All Purpose Flour*
2 teaspoons baking powder
½ teaspoon seasoned salt
½ teaspoon basil
¾ cup heavy cream

OVEN 425°　　　　　　　4 TO 6 SERVINGS

Place peas, onions and milk in 1½-quart casserole. Cover and bake at 425° for 15 to 20 minutes. Remove from oven. Stir in minced clams. Drop Biscuits by tablespoonfuls onto casserole. Bake uncovered at 425° for 30 to 35 minutes.

Biscuits: In mixing bowl, combine flour, baking powder, seasoned salt and basil. Add cream, stirring until dry particles are moistened.

Tip: Use clam liquid for part of milk in filling.

*For use with Pillsbury's Best Self-Rising Flour, omit baking powder and seasoned salt.

Salmon has never been so well dressed as it is with this elegant cucumber sauce. Do it in about an hour and a quarter and boost your stock as a gourmet cook.

Gourmet Salmon Pie

9-inch Unbaked Pastry Shell, see page 5

    10-ounce package frozen cut asparagus
    3 eggs, beaten
    2 tablespoons milk
    2 tablespoons butter, melted
    1 teaspoon dried parsley flakes
    ¼ teaspoon salt
    1-pound can salmon, drained, flaked and
      boned

Topping

    ⅓ cup finely chopped cucumber
    8-ounce carton sour cream with chives
    2 teaspoons dried parsley flakes
    2 teaspoons vinegar
    ⅛ teaspoon salt
    ¹/₁₆ teaspoon pepper

OVEN 425°   5 TO 6 SERVINGS

Cook asparagus as directed on package; drain. Combine eggs, milk, butter, parsley and salt. Add salmon and asparagus. Stir only until blended. Pour into prepared Unbaked Pastry Shell. Bake at 425° for 20 to 25 minutes. Prepare Topping. Spread Topping around edge of baked pie. Return to oven for 5 minutes. Serve hot.

Topping: Combine cucumber, chive sour cream, parsley flakes, vinegar, salt and pepper. Mix well.

Create a delightful new flavor experience with apples in a lamb curry. A two hour recipe.

Apple Lamb Casserole

    1 pound cubed lamb shoulder
    ⅓ cup Pillsbury's Best All Purpose or
      Self-Rising Flour
    2 tablespoons shortening
    2 cups water
    1 large bay leaf
    1 teaspoon salt
    1 teaspoon dried parsley flakes
    ½ teaspoon thyme
    ¼ to ½ teaspoon curry powder
    ⅛ teaspoon pepper
    1 small whole onion
    1-pound 4-ounce can sliced pie apples
    2 tablespoons sugar
    1 can Pillsbury Refrigerated Hungry Jack
      Flaky or Flaky Buttermilk Biscuits

OVEN 425°   5 TO 6 SERVINGS

Coat lamb with flour. Brown in shortening in large skillet. Stir in water, bay leaf, salt, parsley flakes, thyme, curry powder, pepper and onion. Cover and simmer 1 hour until meat is tender, stirring occasionally. Remove onion and bay leaf. Stir in apples and sugar. Bring to a boil. Turn into 8 or 9-inch square baking dish. Open can; separate dough into 10 biscuits. Place around edge of baking dish. Bake at 425° for 15 to 18 minutes.

Tip: If desired, use 3 cups diced fresh pared apples. Add to meat mixture last 20 minutes of simmer time.

Sweet Cherry Ham Bake

Ham chunks glazed with spicy pie cherries, topped with parkerhouse biscuits. A pretty Christmas supper, ready in about an hour and a quarter.

Sweet Cherry Ham Bake

  4 cups cubed cooked ham
  1 cup chopped celery
  ½ teaspoon dry mustard
  1-pound can prepared cherry pie filling
  2 tablespoons brown sugar
  3 tablespoons lemon juice
  ⅛ teaspoon ground cloves

Parkerhouse Biscuits
  1½ cups Pillsbury's Best All Purpose Flour*
  1 tablespoon sugar
  2 teaspoons baking powder
  ½ teaspoon salt
  ¼ cup shortening
  ⅓ cup milk
  1 egg
  1 to 2 tablespoons butter

OVEN 425°   6 SERVINGS

Combine ham, celery and dry mustard in 12x8-inch baking dish. Combine cherry pie filling, brown sugar, lemon juice and cloves. Spoon over ham. Bake at 425° for 20 minutes. Place Parkerhouse Biscuits on hot mixture. Bake at 425° for 15 to 20 minutes until golden brown.

Parkerhouse Biscuits: Combine dry ingredients in mixing bowl. Cut in shortening. Combine milk and egg. Add to dry ingredients; mix until dry particles are moistened. Knead on floured surface 12 strokes. Roll biscuits to ¼-inch thickness. Cut into rounds with floured 2½-inch cutter. Make a crease with dull edge of knife to one side of center. Place small pat of butter on larger portion. Fold small portion over butter; press to seal.

Tip: If desired, use 1 can Pillsbury Refrigerated Quick Parkerhouse Dinner Rolls for Parkerhouse Biscuits. Bake at 400° for 15 to 20 minutes.

*For use with Pillsbury's Best Self-Rising Flour, omit baking powder and salt.

Ham, sweet potatoes and pineapple all decked out in a bright new flavor — cranberry. Table-ready in an hour and a half.

Cranberry Whirl Ham Dinner

  3 cups cubed cooked ham
  2 cups sliced cooked sweet potatoes
13½-ounce can pineapple chunks, drained, reserving juice
  ½ cup whole cranberry sauce
  2 tablespoons plus ¼ cup firmly packed brown sugar
  1 tablespoon flour
  ½ teaspoon cinnamon
  ⅛ teaspoon ground cloves

OVEN 375°   6 TO 8 SERVINGS

Place half of ham, sweet potatoes and pineapple chunks in layers in 1½-quart casserole. Spoon half of cranberry sauce, by teaspoonfuls over casserole. Repeat layers. Combine 2 tablespoons brown sugar, flour, cinnamon and cloves in small saucepan. Blend in ½ cup reserved pineapple juice. Cook over medium heat until mixture boils. Pour over mixture in casserole. Sprinkle with ¼ cup brown sugar. Bake uncovered at 375° for 50 to 60 minutes.

Sweet potatoes and yams are available in different areas. Yams are sweeter, deeper in color, and softer textured than sweet potatoes. In most recipes one can be substituted for the other depending on your taste preference.

Cheesy quick croutons from refrigerated biscuits accompany this crowd-pleasing southern gumbo, easy-made with prepared foods in less than one and a half hours.

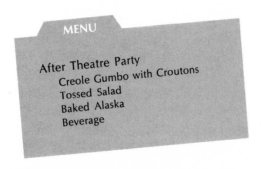

MENU

After Theatre Party
Creole Gumbo with Croutons
Tossed Salad
Baked Alaska
Beverage

Both subtle and savory, crisp and tender, this casserole scores high with cantonese food enthusiasts. Quickly prepared in thirty minutes.

Cantonese Casserole

    I pound pork tenderloin, cut in thin ½-inch strips
  ½ cup thin sliced green pepper
  ¼ cup chopped onion
  2 tablespoons shortening
  I-pound can bean sprouts, drained
10½-ounce can cream of mushroom soup
  8-ounce can tomato sauce
  I tablespoon vinegar
  I teaspoon sugar
  2 teaspoons Worcestershire sauce
  ½ teaspoon celery salt
  ⅛ teaspoon pepper
  3 cups cooked rice
  I teaspoon butter

5 TO 6 SERVINGS

Brown pork, green pepper and onion in shortening in large skillet. Stir in remaining ingredients except rice and butter. Simmer, covered, 25 to 30 minutes until meat is tender. Prepare rice; add butter. Arrange on serving platter or in serving dish; pour meat mixture in center.

Creole Gumbo

  I cup chopped celery
  ½ cup chopped onion
  ½ cup chopped green pepper
  2 cloves garlic, minced
  3 tablespoons olive or cooking oil
  2 tablespoons flour
  I-pound can tomatoes
  8-ounce can tomato sauce
  I tablespoon Worcestershire sauce
  2 teaspoons salt
  10-ounce package frozen okra,* partially thawed, and cut in ½-inch slices
  7-ounce package frozen shrimp, partially thawed
  6-ounce package frozen crabmeat, partially thawed
  ¼ cup cooking sherry
  I tablespoon dried parsley flakes

Cheesy Quick Croutons
  I can Pillsbury Hungry Jack Flaky or Flaky Buttermilk Biscuits
  Milk
  ¼ cup grated Parmesan cheese
  2 tablespoons corn meal

OVEN 400°   6 TO 8 SERVINGS

Sauté celery, onion, green pepper and garlic in oil in large saucepan until tender, about 10 minutes. Stir in flour, cook until bubbly. Blend in tomatoes, tomato sauce, Worcestershire sauce and salt. Cover and simmer for 45 minutes to I hour. Add okra, shrimp, crabmeat, sherry and parsley. Simmer for 20 minutes more. Serve in bowls with Cheesy Quick Croutons.

Cheesy Quick Croutons: Open can; separate dough into 10 biscuits. Cut each biscuit into quarters. Dip in milk, then roll in mixture of Parmesan cheese and corn meal. Place on ungreased cookie sheet. Bake at 400° for 8 to 10 minutes until golden brown.

Tips: For cheesy quick biscuits, leave biscuits *whole. Dip in milk and cheese mixture. Bake as directed on label.*

Prepare gumbo ahead. Cool, cover and refrigerate. Reheat just before serving.

*If desired, use I-pound can sliced okra, undrained.

A delicious surprise rolled up in delicate crepes and topped with a sherried sour cream sauce. Prepare these ahead of time and refrigerate or allow one and a half hours.

Chicken Filled Crepes

    4 eggs
  1⅓ cups milk
   ½ teaspoon salt
   I cup Pillsbury's Best All Purpose or
      Self-Rising Flour
   ¼ cup slivered almonds

Filling

   3 cups cubed cooked chicken
   II-ounce can mandarin oranges, drained
   5-ounce can water chestnuts, drained and
      finely chopped
   ¼ cup mayonnaise
   ½ teaspoon salt

Topping

   ½ cup dairy sour cream
   ¼ cup mayonnaise
   2 tablespoons cooking sherry

OVEN 375°   5 TO 6 SERVINGS

Combine eggs, milk and salt in medium mixing bowl with rotary beater. Add flour, beat until smooth. Heat a 7 or 8-inch skillet over medium heat. (Be sure pan is hot before starting.) Grease lightly before each crepe. Pour batter, scant ¼ cup at a time, into skillet tilting pan to spread evenly. When crepe is light brown and set, turn to brown other side. Spread about ⅓ cup Filling down center of each crepe; roll up. Place seam side down in a I2x8-inch or I3x9-inch baking dish. Pour Topping back and forth over crepes. Sprinkle with almonds. Bake at 375° for 20 to 25 minutes.

<u>Filling:</u> Combine all ingredients.

<u>Topping:</u> Fold sour cream, mayonnaise and sherry together.

Tip: Prepare ahead, cover and refrigerate. Bake at 350° for 30 to 35 minutes.

Even the biscuit topping has the East Indian touch. Give yourself two and a half hours to make this extraordinary recipe, for your most adventurous friends.

Calcutta Lamb Curry Casserole

   3 tablespoons butter
   2 pounds lamb shoulder, cut into 1-inch
      cubes
⅓ cup Pillsbury's Best All Purpose or
      Self-Rising Flour
   ¼ cup instant minced onion
   1 tablespoon curry powder
   ½ teaspoon instant minced garlic
   9-ounce jar chutney, drained, reserving
      liquid
13¾-ounce can (2 cups) chicken broth
   1 cup diced tart apples
   1 cup chopped celery
   2 teaspoons salt

Biscuits

   1½ cups Pillsbury's Best All Purpose Flour*
   2 teaspoons baking powder
   ½ teaspoon salt
   ½ teaspoon mace
   ⅓ cup flaked coconut
   ¼ cup butter
   ½ cup milk
   ⅓ cup raisins
   2 tablespoons diced roasted almonds

OVEN 350°   8 SERVINGS

Place butter in 2½-quart casserole; place in oven to melt. Add lamb, flour, onion, curry powder and garlic; mix well. Bake uncovered at 350° for 30 minutes. Remove from oven. Blend reserved chutney liquid into meat mixture with chicken broth, apples, celery and salt. (Reserved chutney will be used in Biscuits.) Bake covered for 1 hour at 350°. Prepare Biscuits. Remove casserole from oven. Increase oven temperature to 425°. Place Biscuits, cut side down, on casserole. Bake uncovered at 425° for 25 to 30 minutes.

Biscuits: Combine flour, baking powder, salt and mace in mixing bowl. Cut in butter until particles are fine. Mix in coconut. Add milk; stir until dough clings together. Knead 12 times on lightly floured surface. Roll out to a 12x10-inch rectangle. Chop chutney; combine with raisins and almonds. Spread over dough. Starting with 12-inch side, roll up jelly roll fashion. Seal edges. Cut into 1-inch slices.

*For use with Pillsbury's Best Self-Rising Flour, omit baking powder and salt.

"Oysters?" you say. Yes, smoked oysters . . . a delicious compliment to leftover turkey. So simple it's table-ready in about forty-five minutes.

Turkey Oyster Triumph

   2 cups cubed cooked turkey
3⅔-ounce can smoked oysters, drained
   ¼ cup finely chopped celery
   1 tablespoon chopped pimiento
   2 teaspoons dried parsley flakes
   1 teaspoon instant minced onion
10½-ounce can condensed cream of
      mushroom soup

Topping

   ½ cup dry bread cubes
   ¼ cup slivered almonds
   1 tablespoon butter, melted

OVEN 400°   4 TO 5 SERVINGS

Combine turkey, oysters, celery, pimiento, parsley, onion and mushroom soup in a greased 1½-quart casserole. Sprinkle with Topping. Bake at 400° for 20 to 25 minutes.

Topping: Combine dry bread cubes, slivered almonds and butter.

Tip: This can be prepared ahead, covered and refrigerated. Bake at 400° for 25 to 30 minutes.

A round lasagna casserole, with delicate pan-cakes replacing the traditional lasagna noodles. A perfect do-ahead dish or allow one and a half hours.

Italian Pancake Casserole

2 eggs
⅔ cup milk
½ cup Pillsbury's Best All Purpose or
    Self-Rising Flour
¼ teaspoon salt
1 pound lean ground beef
6-ounce can tomato paste
2 tablespoons instant minced onion
1 teaspoon basil
¾ teaspoon garlic salt
½ teaspoon oregano
½ teaspoon salt
¼ teaspoon pepper
1 cup creamed cottage cheese
2 cups (½ pound) shredded Mozzarella
    cheese
¼ cup grated Parmesan cheese

OVEN 375°   5 TO 6 SERVINGS

Combine eggs and milk in medium mixing bowl with rotary beater. Add flour and salt; beat until smooth. Heat a 9-inch skillet over medium high heat. Grease lightly before baking each pancake. Pour batter, ⅓ cup at a time, into skillet tilting pan to spread evenly over bottom. When pancake is light brown and set, turn to brown other side. Prepare 4 pancakes.

Brown ground beef in medium skillet; add tomato paste, onion, basil, garlic salt, oregano, salt and pepper. Place one pancake on bottom of 10-inch pie pan, 9-inch round cake pan or 9-inch skillet. Spread with ¼ cup cottage cheese, ¼ meat mixture, ½ cup shredded Mozzarella cheese and 1 tablespoon grated Parmesan cheese. Repeat with remaining pancakes ending with cheese. Bake at 375° for 30 to 35 minutes. To serve, cut in wedges.

Tip: Refrigerate up to 24 hours. Bake for 35 to 40 minutes.

129

The crunch of water chestnuts and fragrance of sherry make it special. Prepare it ahead in less than an hour, and serve over pretty rings of toast.

Sea King Dinner

½ cup chopped green pepper
½ cup chopped onion
½ cup chopped celery
¼ cup butter
¼ cup Pillsbury's Best All Purpose or
   Self-Rising Flour
½ teaspoon garlic salt
½ teaspoon salt
¼ teaspoon paprika
$^1/_{16}$ teaspoon cayenne pepper
   4-ounce can mushroom stems and pieces,
      undrained
   7-ounce package frozen shrimp
   6-ounce package frozen crabmeat
   5-ounce can water chestnuts, drained and
      sliced
⅓ cup cooking sherry
   I cup shredded Cheddar cheese

Toast Puffs
   16 slices bread
   ¼ cup butter, melted

OVEN 375°   6 TO 8 SERVINGS

Sauté green pepper, onion and celery in butter in large saucepan until tender, about 10 minutes. Blend in flour, garlic salt, salt, paprika and cayenne pepper. Cook until bubbly. Blend in mushrooms, shrimp, crabmeat, water chestnuts and sherry. Simmer, covered, 20 minutes. Blend in cheese stirring until melted. Serve over Toast Puffs or patty shells.

Toast Puffs: Cut sixteen 2½-inch circles from bread slices. Dip one side of 8 circles in butter and place buttered side up on ungreased cookie sheet. Cut ½-inch hole in center of remaining circles (doughnut cutter works very well). Dip outside ring in butter. Place on top of base, buttered side up. Bake at 375° for 10 to 12 minutes until golden brown.

Tips: Keep hot over water in chafing dish.

Prepare seafood mixture ahead; reheat just before serving. Prepare Toast Puffs ahead and cover. Bake just before serving.

MENU
Buffet Luncheon Party
   Sea King Dinner
   Buttered Broccoli
   Frozen Fruit Salad on Lettuce Cup
   Brownie A La Mode
   Beverage

A crunchy crabmeat mixture hidden between a pastry crust and cheesy sauce. A delicious dish in an hour and a quarter.

Down East Crabmeat Pie

8-inch Unbaked Pastry Shell, see page 5

  7¼-ounce can crabmeat, drained and flaked
  ⅔ cup chopped celery
  ⅓ cup chopped green pepper
  ⅓ cup chili sauce
  2 tablespoons flour
  1 tablespoon instant minced onion
  ½ teaspoon salt
  2 teaspoons Worcestershire sauce
  ¼ cup shredded Swiss cheese
    Paprika

Sauce
  2 tablespoons butter
  2 tablespoons flour
  ¼ teaspoon salt
  ¾ cup milk
  ¾ cup shredded Swiss cheese
  2 tablespoons cooking sherry, if desired

OVEN 400°   6 SERVINGS

Combine crabmeat, celery, green pepper, chili sauce, flour, onion, salt and Worcestershire sauce in mixing bowl. Spoon into Unbaked Pastry Shell. Pour Sauce over filling, spreading to cover. Sprinkle with ¼ cup shredded cheese and paprika. Bake at 400° for 20 to 25 minutes until bubbly and golden brown. Let cool 10 minutes before cutting in wedges and serving.

Sauce: Melt butter in small saucepan. Blend in flour and salt; cook until bubbly. Gradually stir in milk. Cook over medium heat until mixture boils and thickens. Remove from heat. Stir in ¾ cup shredded cheese and sherry.

Soda crackers provide the topping for these little crabmeat filled custard squares, mounted on a biscuity crust. Give yourself an hour and a half to prepare.

Crab-In-A-Custard

  1 cup Pillsbury's Best All Purpose Flour*
  1½ teaspoons salt
  1 teaspoon baking powder
  1 teaspoon sugar
  3 tablespoons butter, softened
  4 eggs
  ½ cup milk
  2 (7½-ounce) cans crabmeat, drained, reserving liquid
  ⅓ cup minced green pepper
  ½ cup shredded Cheddar cheese
  1¾ cups light cream
  ¼ cup white cooking wine
  2 teaspoons Worcestershire sauce
  16 soda crackers
    Pepper

OVEN 350°   8 SERVINGS

In small mixer bowl combine flour, 1 teaspoon salt, baking powder, sugar, 2 tablespoons butter, 1 egg and milk. Mix at low speed of mixer until smooth, about 1½ minutes. Spread in bottom of greased 9-inch square baking dish. Drain crabmeat, reserving liquid; flake. Spread crabmeat and green pepper evenly over dough; sprinkle with cheese. Combine reserved crabmeat liquid, cream, white cooking wine, Worcestershire sauce, ½ teaspoon salt and 3 eggs. Beat until smooth and well blended. Pour gently over crab mixture. Spread crackers with 1 tablespoon butter. Place on top of sauce; press each cracker into sauce just to moisten tops. Sprinkle with pepper. Bake at 350° for 45 to 50 minutes until sauce is set and golden brown. Let stand 10 minutes before serving.

Tip: If desired, omit cooking wine and substitute ¼ cup light cream.

*For use with Pillsbury's Best Self-Rising Flour, omit salt and baking powder.

MENU

Dinner Party
Continental Steak Rolls
Sour Cream Mashed Potatoes
Brussels Sprouts
Lettuce Wedges with Blue Cheese Dressing
Cherries Jubilee over Ice Cream
Beverage

Sweet and sour ham under a nut-studded topping. Ready for your private luau in just about an hour.

Polynesian Casserole

13½-ounce can pineapple tidbits, drained,
    reserving liquid
  3 cups cubed cooked ham or luncheon
    meat
  2 cups sliced cooked sweet potatoes
  ⅓ cup firmly packed brown sugar
  ¼ cup flour
  ¼ teaspoon curry powder
  ⅛ teaspoon pepper
    Water
  2 tablespoons vinegar

Topping

  1 cup Pillsbury's Best All Purpose Flour*
  2 teaspoons sugar
  2 teaspoons baking powder
  ¼ teaspoon salt
  ½ cup chopped Macadamia nuts or almonds
  ½ cup milk
  2 eggs, separated
  2 tablespoons butter, melted

OVEN 375°   6 TO 8 SERVINGS

Layer pineapple, ham and sweet potatoes in 2-quart casserole. Combine brown sugar, flour, curry powder and pepper. Add water to reserved pineapple syrup to make 1 cup. Blend into brown sugar mixture with vinegar. Pour over casserole. Bake at 375° for 20 minutes. Pour Topping over casserole, spreading to cover. Bake 20 to 25 minutes longer or until golden brown.

Topping: Combine flour, sugar, baking powder, salt and nuts in mixing bowl. Blend milk, egg yolks and butter. Add to dry ingredients. Stir just until moistened. Beat egg whites until stiff, but not dry. Fold into batter.

*For use with Pillsbury's Best Self-Rising Flour, omit baking powder and salt.

Individual steak rolls come to dinner with sherry stuffing, in a mushroom-almond sauce. Allow three hours.

Continental Steak Rolls

  2 cups soft bread cubes
  ¼ cup chopped ripe olives
  ⅓ cup cooking sherry or beef bouillon
  1 teaspoon onion salt
  1 teaspoon Worcestershire sauce
  ¼ teaspoon pepper
  2 pounds round steak, ½-inch thick
  ¼ cup Pillsbury's Best All Purpose or
    Self-Rising Flour
  ½ teaspoon salt
  ½ teaspoon garlic salt
  ¼ cup slivered almonds
10½-ounce can condensed cream of
    mushroom soup
  ½ cup milk
  ⅛ teaspoon nutmeg

OVEN 350°   6 SERVINGS

Combine bread cubes, olives, sherry, onion salt, Worcestershire sauce, and pepper. Cut round steak into 6 serving pieces. Coat with mixture of flour, salt and garlic salt. Top each piece with 1/6 of stuffing. Bring opposite edges around stuffing to meet. Hold together with toothpicks. Place seamside down in greased shallow 2-quart casserole. Sprinkle with almonds. Bake uncovered at 350° for 30 minutes. Remove from oven. Combine soup, milk and nutmeg. Pour over steak rolls. Cover and bake 2 hours longer until meat is tender. Serve on platter with sauce. Garnish with fresh snipped parsley, if desired.

Tip: Prepare meat rolls early in day. Cover and refrigerate until 2½ to 3 hours before serving.

Continental Steak Rolls

Onion-lovers arise! It takes about an hour and a quarter to prepare this cheese-topped onion custard filling in its caraway crust.

Caraway Onion Pie

9-inch Unbaked Pastry Shell, see page 5
  1 tablespoon caraway seed

Filling
  4 cups (12-ounce package) frozen chopped
    onion
  2 tablespoons butter

Topping
  2 tablespoons flour
  1½ teaspoons salt
  ¼ teaspoon paprika
  ½ cup grated Parmesan cheese
  3 eggs
  1¼ cups milk

OVEN 400°   5 TO 6 SERVINGS

Prepare pastry for 9-inch Unbaked Pastry Shell as directed on page 5, adding 1 tablespoon caraway seed to the flour or pie crust mix or stick. Place Filling in bottom of Unbaked Pastry Shell. Pour Topping over Filling. Bake at 400° for 35 to 40 minutes until golden brown.

Filling: Combine frozen onions and butter in covered saucepan. Steam, covered, for 10 to 15 minutes over low heat until tender.

Topping: Combine flour, salt, paprika and Parmesan cheese. Add eggs and milk. Mix well.

A marvelous main-dish veal pizza in a distinctive herb crust. Beautiful to serve in an hour and a half.

Venetian Veal Pie

  1 pound veal round steak, cut in strips
  ⅓ cup Pillsbury's Best All Purpose or
    Self-Rising Flour
  3 tablespoons olive or cooking oil
  ½ cup white cooking wine
  8-ounce can tomato sauce
  ¼ cup chopped onion
  1 tablespoon sugar
  1 teaspoon basil
  ½ teaspoon salt
  ½ teaspoon garlic salt
  ½ teaspoon leaf oregano
  ⅛ teaspoon pepper
  1 cup shredded Mozzarella cheese
  3 tablespoons grated Parmesan or
    Romano cheese

Pie Crust
  8-inch Unbaked Pastry Shell
  ¼ cup grated Parmesan or Romano cheese
  1 teaspoon leaf oregano
  ½ teaspoon garlic salt

OVEN 450°   5 SERVINGS

Coat veal with flour. Brown in oil in large skillet, adding all the flour. Reduce heat; add wine. Mix well. Add tomato sauce, onion, sugar, basil, salt, garlic salt, oregano and pepper. Simmer, covered, for 30 minutes or until meat is tender.

Meanwhile prepare recipe for 8-inch Unbaked Pastry Shell as directed on page 5 adding cheese, oregano and garlic salt to flour or pie crust mix or stick. Bake as directed at 450°. Remove from oven; reduce oven temperature to 350°. Pour hot filling into crust. Sprinkle with Mozzarella and Parmesan cheese. Bake at 350° for 10 minutes until cheese is melted. Let cool 10 minutes before cutting in wedges and serving.

Your mild flavored meats such as veal, chicken and fish, are enhanced by adding white wines. Red wine is the perfect partner for beef dishes.

The tang of mustard compliments the crab in this light and lovely dish that can be your party triumph in an hour and a half.

Fancy Fish Soufflé

3 tablespoons dry bread crumbs
⅓ cup butter
½ cup Pillsbury's Best All Purpose or
    Self-Rising Flour
1¼ teaspoons salt
¼ teaspoon dry mustard
1¾ cups milk
¼ cup cooking sherry
½ teaspoon Worcestershire sauce
7¼-ounce can crabmeat, drained and flaked
4 eggs, separated

OVEN 350°   4 TO 6 SERVINGS

Grease a 1½-quart casserole or soufflé dish. Sprinkle with 2 tablespoons bread crumbs. Set aside. Melt butter in medium saucepan. Add flour, salt and mustard. Cook until bubbly. Gradually stir in milk. Cook, stirring constantly, until mixture boils. Stir in cooking sherry, Worcestershire sauce and crabmeat. Bring just to boil. Beat egg yolks slightly. Blend a little of hot mixture into yolks. Add to remaining hot mixture, blend well. Beat egg whites until stiff but not dry. Fold into hot mixture. Pour into baking dish. Sprinkle remaining tablespoon of crumbs over top. Set in pan containing 1-inch hot water. Bake at 350° for 45 to 50 minutes until knife inserted in center comes out clean.

Tip: If desired, use 7¼-ounce can drained lobster meat in place of crabmeat.

HIGH ALTITUDE ADJUSTMENT — 5,200 FEET.
Bake at 350° for 55 to 60 minutes.

The star of this paprika veal stew is the butter crumb dumplings, like floating puffs of dressing. An hour and a quarter dish.

California Casserole

2 pounds veal round steak, cut in 1-inch
    pieces
⅓ cup Pillsbury's Best All Purpose or
    Self-Rising Flour
1 teaspoon paprika
¼ cup cooking oil
½ teaspoon salt
⅛ teaspoon pepper
2¼ cups water
10½-ounce can condensed cream of chicken
    soup
1-pound can small cooked onions, drained

Butter Crumb Dumplings
2 cups Pillsbury's Best All Purpose Flour*
1 tablespoon poppy seed, if desired
4 teaspoons baking powder
1 teaspoon poultry seasoning
1 teaspoon celery seed
1 teaspoon instant minced onion
½ teaspoon salt
¼ cup cooking oil
1 cup milk
¼ cup butter, melted
1 cup dry bread crumbs

OVEN 425°   6 TO 8 SERVINGS

Coat veal with mixture of flour and paprika; brown in oil in large skillet. Add salt, pepper and 1 cup water (part onion liquid may be used). Cover; simmer 30 minutes or until tender. Transfer to a 3-quart casserole. Heat soup in skillet used for browning meat. Gradually blend in 1¼ cups water. Bring to a boil, stirring constantly. Combine with meat and gravy. Add onions. Top with Butter Crumb Dumplings. Bake uncovered at 425° for 20 to 25 minutes until golden brown.

Butter Crumb Dumplings: Combine flour, poppy seed, baking powder, poultry seasoning, celery seed, onion and salt in large mixing bowl. Add oil and milk. Stir just until moistened. Drop rounded tablespoonfuls of dough into mixture of butter and bread crumbs; roll to coat well with crumbs.

*For use with Pillsbury's Best Self-Rising Flour, omit baking powder and salt.

Cheese and wine fondue, with newsworthy little squares of potato-and-sesame yeast bread. Make bread ahead, fondue in the final thirty minutes.

Fun-Do Fondue

Bread

    1 package active dry yeast
    1 cup warm water
    1 cup Pillsbury Hungry Jack Mashed
       Potato Flakes
    1 tablespoon sugar
    2 tablespoons cooking oil
    1 teaspoon salt
    1 egg
  1¾ to 2 cups Pillsbury's Best All Purpose
       Flour*
    3 tablespoons sesame seed
     Milk

Fondue

    4 cups (1-pound) shredded Swiss cheese
    ¼ cup flour
    ¼ teaspoon salt
    ¼ teaspoon nutmeg
     Dash of pepper
    1 clove garlic
    2 cups white cooking wine
    2 tablespoons kirch, if desired

MENU

Apres Ski Party
   Fun-do Fondue
   Tossed Salad
   Fresh Fruits 'n Dip
   Applesauce-Spice Cake
   Beverage

OVEN 400°   6 SERVINGS

<u>Bread</u>: Soften yeast in warm water. Blend in potato flakes, sugar, oil, salt and egg. Add flour gradually to form a stiff dough. Knead on floured surface until smooth, about 1 minute. Place in greased bowl. Cover; let rise in warm place until light and doubled, about 1 hour. Sprinkle 1 tablespoon sesame seed on greased cookie sheet. Place dough on cookie sheet and roll out to 14x10-inch rectangle. Brush with milk; sprinkle with 2 tablespoons sesame seed. Cover; let rise until light, about 45 minutes. Bake at 400° for 15 to 18 minutes until golden brown. Remove to cooling rack. Cool. Cut into 1-inch squares.

<u>Fondue</u>: Combine cheese, flour, salt, nutmeg and pepper. Cut garlic and rub over inside of earthenware fondue dish or chafing dish. Add wine and heat over direct heat. When tiny bubbles begin rising from bottom, begin adding cheese, handful at a time, stirring vigorously until cheese begins to melt and blend in. Continue until all cheese is melted and thoroughly blended. Stir in kirch. Serve immediately by spearing squares of bread with fork and dipping into the Fondue.

<u>Tips</u>: *Fondue must be kept hot while being served, so use some kind of dish that can be served over a heating unit at the table.*

If Fondue becomes too thick, stir in a little more warm wine.

*For use with Pillsbury's Best Self-Rising Flour, omit salt.

Under the rich red tomato sauce are golden corn pancakes with a Spanish-speaking ground beef mixture inside. These can be made ahead.

Enchiladas

Tortillas
>2 cups cold water
>2 eggs
>I cup corn meal
>I cup Pillsbury's Best All Purpose Flour*
>¼ teaspoon salt

Filling
>I pound lean ground beef
>½ cup chopped onion
>½ teaspoon salt
>½ teaspoon garlic salt
>½ to I teaspoon chili powder

Tomato Sauce
>I cup chopped onion
>I tablespoon cooking oil
>2 (8-ounce) cans tomato sauce
>I teaspoon chili powder
>½ teaspoon salt
>½ teaspoon garlic salt
>¼ teaspoon hot pepper sauce
>2 cups shredded Cheddar cheese

OVEN 350°   6 SERVINGS

With rotary beater combine water and eggs. Add corn meal, flour and salt; beat until smooth. Pour ¼ cup batter into a hot greased 7 or 8-inch skillet, tilting to spread. Cook until top is set and loses gloss (2 to 3 minutes). Remove with spatula. Repeat to make I2 tortillas. Place one equal portion Filling on each tortilla; roll up and place in ungreased I3x9-inch baking pan. Pour Tomato Sauce over tortillas; sprinkle with cheese. Bake at 350° for 55 to 60 minutes.

Filling: Combine all ingredients. Divide into twelve equal portions.

Tomato Sauce: In skillet sauté onion in oil until tender. Stir in tomato sauce, chili powder, salt, garlic salt and hot pepper sauce.

Tips: These can be made ahead, covered and refrigerated until ready to bake.

For quick tortillas, use a package of I2 frozen or canned tortillas. Prepare as directed on package and then fill as directed.

*For use with Pillsbury's Best Self-Rising Flour, omit salt.

"Chow mein meat" as found in the fresh meat counter usually contains a combination of pork and veal cut in small pieces.

A delicious chow mein, with the hearty touch of brown gravy that makes it different. Ring the dinner gong in an hour.

Shanghai Casserole

>½ pound boneless pork, cut in small thin strips
>½ pound boneless veal, cut in small thin strips
>3 tablespoons flour
>2 tablespoons cooking oil
>I package Pillsbury Brown Gravy Mix
>3 tablespoons soy sauce
>4-ounce can mushroom stems and pieces, undrained
>I-pound can chow mein vegetables, undrained
>I½ cups sliced celery
>I medium onion, sliced
>4 to 5 cups chow mein noodles

OVEN 350°   6 SERVINGS

Coat pork and veal with flour. Brown meat in oil in large skillet. Add gravy mix, soy sauce, mushrooms, and liquid from chow mein vegetables. Cover and simmer 30 minutes. Add celery, onion and chow mein vegetables. Cover and simmer I0 to I5 minutes longer until vegetables are tender. Pour into shallow casserole or serving dish. Arrange noodles around edge. Serve.

This is an excellent stroganoff, topped with two-layer sour cream puffs. It makes its dramatic appearance in less than two and a half hours.

Strips of Beef Casserole

1½ pounds round steak, cut into ½-inch
    strips
1½ cups chopped onion
3 tablespoons flour
1½ teaspoons salt
6-ounce can tomato paste
1 cup (8-ounces) tomatoes
4-ounce can mushroom stems and pieces,
    drained
½ cup water
1 tablespoon sugar
½ teaspoon Worcestershire sauce
¾ cup dairy sour cream
2 teaspoons sesame seed

Sour Cream Biscuits
1¼ cups Pillsbury's Best All Purpose Flour*
2 teaspoons baking powder
½ teaspoon salt
¼ cup shortening
¾ cup dairy sour cream

OVEN 350°   6 TO 8 SERVINGS

Place steak strips and onion in 2-quart casserole. Sprinkle with flour and salt. Toss lightly to coat meat. Bake uncovered at 350° for 30 minutes. Stir in tomato paste, tomatoes, mushrooms, water, sugar and Worcestershire sauce. Cover and bake at 350° for 1½ hours. Remove from oven; increase temperature to 425°. Stir in sour cream. Top with large Sour Cream Biscuits; brush with milk and top each large biscuit with small biscuit. Sprinkle with sesame seed. Bake uncovered at 425° for 20 to 25 minutes. Let stand 10 to 15 minutes before serving.

Sour Cream Biscuits: Combine flour, baking powder and salt. Cut in shortening until particles are fine. Stir in sour cream until dough clings together. Knead lightly on floured surface 8 times. Roll out to ½-inch thickness, cut into 2½-inch rounds and an equal number of 1-inch rounds.

Tip: To prepare ahead, complete to the adding of sour cream. Cool; cover and refrigerate. Place in 350° oven covered for 20 minutes; then add sour cream and continue as directed.

*For use with Pillsbury's Best Self-Rising Flour, omit baking powder and salt.

Index